The Gospel of Thomas

The Original 21-Chapter Poetic Arrangement

Standard Edition

ROBERT W. NORTH, PhD

The Soul Way
www.7771.org

The Gospel of Thomas

The Original 21-Chapter Poetic Arrangement

Standard Edition

Copyright © 2017 by Robert W. North

All rights reserved. No part of this book may be used or reproduced by any means, graphic, electronic, or mechanical, including photocopying, recording, taping or by any information storage retrieval system without the written permission of the publisher except in the case of brief quotations embodied in critical articles and reviews.

To Contact the Author
www.7771.org

Because of the dynamic nature of the Internet, any Web addresses or links contained in this book may have changed since publication and may no longer be valid.

Cover Design

Rishabh Kushwaha
www.creatronicsstudio.com

Book Design

Front Margin
www.frontmargin.com

ISBN-13: 978-0-9907795-5-1

The Soul Way

www.7771.org

Dedication

To a man who embodies this book
And
Without whom it would not be
Mi Querido Amigo

Donald Talarico

CONTENTS

Preface 1

Preliminary: The Discovery of the Gospel of Thomas 37

Introduction 45

Chapter 11
(Sayings 44–50)

Poem 4
(48) P. 155

Poem 3   ←↑→   Poem 5
(46) P. 155   (47) P. 155

Poem 2   ←↑→   Poem 6
(45) P. 158   (49) P. 158

Poem 1   ←↑→   Poem 7
(44) P. 159   (50) P. 159

Chapter 10   ←↑→   **Chapter 12**
(Sayings 39–43)   (Sayings 51–60)

Poem 3   Poem 5   ←→   Poem 6
(41) P. 145   (55) P. 149   (56) P. 149

Poem 2   ←↑→   Poem 4   Poem 4   ←→   Poem 7
(40) P. 145   (42) P. 145   (54) P. 149   (57) P. 149

Poem 1   ←↑→   Poem 5   Poem 3   ←→   Poem 8
(39) P. 146   (43) P. 146   (53) P. 151   (58) P. 151

                                                 Poem 2   ←→   Poem 9
                                                 (52) P. 151   (59) P. 151

                                                 Poem 1   ←→   Poem 10
                                                 (51) P. 153   (60) P. 153

v

Chapter 9
(Sayings 34–38)

Poem 3
(35) P. 137

Poem 2
(36) P. 138

←↑→

Poem 4
(37) P. 138

Poem 1
(34) P. 139

←↑→

Poem 5
(38) P. 139 L

Chapter 8
(Sayings 25–33)

Poem 5
(31) P. 123

Poem 4
(29) P. 124

←↑→

Poem 6
(30) P. 124

Poem 3
(27) P. 125

←↑→

Poem 7
(28) P. 125

Poem 2
(25) P. 127

←↑→

Poem 8
(26) P. 127

Poem 1
(32) P. 128

←↑→

Poem 9
(33) P. 128 L

Chapter 7
(Sayings 22–24)

Poem 2
(23) P. 117

Poem 1
(22) P. 118

←↑→

Poem 3
(24) P. 118 E

Chapter 6
(Sayings 20–21)

Poem 3
(21b) P. 103

Poem 2
(21a) P. 103

←↑→

Poem 4
(21c) P. 103

Poem 1
(20) P. 106

←↑→

Poem 5
(21d) P. 106 E

Chapter 13
(Sayings 61–63)

Poem 3
(62b) P. 141

Poem 2
(61) P. 142

←↑→

Poem 4
(63a) P. 142

Poem 1
(62a) P. 144

←↑→

Poem 5
(63b) P. 144 E

Chapter 14
(Sayings 64–65)

Poem 2
(65b) P. 129

Poem 1
(64) P. 132

←↑→

Poem 3
(65a) P. 132 E

Chapter 15
(Sayings 66–68)

Poem 2
(67) P. 121

Poem 1
(66) P. 122

←↑→

Poem 3
(68) P. 122

Chapter 16
(Sayings 64–65)

Poem 6
(73) P. 109

←→

Poem 7
(74) P. 109

Poem 5
(72) P. 110

←→

Poem 8
(75) P. 110

Poem 4
(71) P. 111

←→

Poem 9
(76) P. 111

Poem 3
(70) P. 113

←→

Poem 10
(77) P. 113

Poem 2
(69a) P. 114

←→

Poem 11
(78) P. 114

Poem 1
(69b) P. 115

←→

Poem 12
(79) P. 115 L

Contents

Chapter 5
(Sayings 18–19)

⇐⇑⇒

Poem 2   ⇐⇒   Poem 3
(18b) P. 95   (19a) P. 95

Poem 1   ⇐⇒   Poem 4
(18a) P. 96   (19b) P. 96 L

Chapter 17
(Sayings 80–87)

Poem 4   ⇐⇒   Poem 5
(83) P. 99   (84) P. 99

Poem 3   ⇐⇒   Poem 6
(82) P. 100   (86) P. 100

Poem 2   ⇐⇒   Poem 7
(81) P. 101   (85) P. 101

Poem 1   ⇐⇒   Poem 8
(80) P. 102   (87) P. 102

Chapter 4
(Sayings 15–17)

⇐⇑⇒

Poem 2
(16) P. 58

Poem 1   ⇐⇑⇒   Poem 3
(15) P. 87   (17) P. 87 L

Chapter 18
(Sayings 88–95)

Poem 4   ⇐⇒   Poem 5
(91) P. 89   (92) P. 89

Poem 3   ⇐⇒   Poem 6
(90) P. 90   (93) P. 90

Poem 2   ⇐⇒   Poem 7
(89) P. 91   (94) P. 91

Poem 1   ⇐⇒   Poem 8
(88) P. 92   (95) P. 92

Chapter 3
(Sayings 9–14)

⇐⇑⇒

Poem 4
(12) P. 71

Poem 3   ⇐⇑⇒   Poem 5
(13) P. 73   (14) P. 73

Poem 2   ⇐⇑⇒   Poem 6
(11a) P. 77   (11b) P. 77

Poem 1   ⇐⇑⇒   Poem 7
(9) P. 78   (10) P. 78

Chapter 19
(Sayings 96–99)

Poem 3
(96b) P. 81

Poem 2   ⇐⇑⇒   Poem 4
(98) P. 82   (99) P. 82

Poem 1   ⇐⇑⇒   Poem 5
(96a) P. 83   (97) P. 83 E

Chapter 2
(Sayings 2–8)

Poem 5
(3b) P. 59

Poem 4 (5) P. 60	←↑→	Poem 6 (6) P. 60
Poem 3 (4) P. 61	←↑→	Poem 7 (7) P. 61
Poem 2 (3a) P. 62	←↑→	Poem 8 (8a) P. 62
Poem 1 (2) P. 64	←↑→	Poem 9 (8b) P. 64 E

←↑→

Chapter 1
(Saying 1)

Poem 1.2
(1) P. 47

Poem 1.1 (1) P. 47	←↑→	Poem 1.3 (1) P. 47

←↑→

Chapter 20
(Sayings 100–105, 107, 112)

Poem 4 (103) P. 67	←↑→	Poem 5 (104) P. 67
Poem 3 (102) P. 68	←↑→	Poem 6 (112) P. 68
Poem 2 (101) P. 69	←↑→	Poem 7 (105) P. 69
Poem 1 (100) P. 70	←↑→	Poem 8 (107) P. 70

Chapter 21
(Sayings 106, 108–111, 113–114)

Poem 5
(111a) P. 53

Poem 4 (110) P. 54	←↑→	Poem 6 (111b) P. 54
Poem 3 (109) P. 55	←↑→	Poem 7 (113) P. 55
Poem 2 (106) P. 57	←↑→	Poem 8 (114) P. 57
Poem 1 (108) P. 58	←↑→	Poem 9 (Ear Poem Missing in the Text) P. 58 E

Appendix One: A Way of the Soul Primer.................................161

Appendix Two: Way of the Soul – Way of the Mind Self-Examination 177

Appendix Three: The Evidence that Jesus is the Author of The Gospel of Thomas 181

Appendix Four: Was Jesus the Expected Messiah.................................185

Acknowledgements..191

PREFACE

This is the "Standard Edition" of the Gospel of Thomas. Available is the much large "Professional Edition" with 200 pages of extra Appendices.

In 1945, some Egyptian farmers discovered a huge, buried vase near Nag Hammadi, Egypt. Historians believe it was hidden by Christian monks in the 4th century, and that it probably contained portions of their library that they wanted to protect and preserve. Among the books was one entitled the "Gospel of Thomas." This Book begins with the remarkable statement that Jesus was the Book's author, speaking its words to a scribe by the name of "Thomas." Within 10 years of its discovery, scholars were able to divide the book into 114 "sayings," about half of which we read in some form in the New Testament. These and later scholars could not find any organization to the book; therefore, they concluded that it was largely a "collection" of sayings put together in the 1st or 2nd century.

About 18 years ago, living in a cabin in the desert outside of Santa Fe, New Mexico, facing a late life "meaning crisis," I sensed that I should fully immerse myself in the study of the Gospel of Thomas. Prior to that, I had studied for the priesthood as a Jesuit to seek and proclaim the real Jesus. However, after many years of deep study, I could not find him or his practical answers to my inner turmoil in Catholic theology.

After I left the Jesuits and after I earned a Ph.D. in Counseling at the University of Florida, I continued with my study of scripture hoping to find "the real Jesus." My Biblical scholarship specialty became the unearthing of the "signals" that ancient Semitic authors imbedded in their writings to tell us how to organize and interpret their works. Our present chapter, verse, paragraph, sentence, and stanza organization was imposed by translators and printers 400 to 500 years ago. When we use the artificial schemes they imposed, we do ***not*** read the text as the original authors intended.

Sitting in my cabin and reading Thomas using the learned ancient "Semitic signals, I could see that it was not a "collection" of sayings as scholars claimed, but a highly organized book. After I read it a second time, I was thrilled to exclaim, "This is the real Jesus. What a revolutionary message! The world needs to hear this now. If everyone lived this Gospel, all religious conflicts would end; and furthermore, I see a way out of my existential crisis!"

And so, with the help of colleagues I have spent years unearthing Jesus' core message in Thomas while cross checking the discoveries with his New Testament parables and main sayings. This is one of a series of books that present the results of our exploratory expedition. Our conclusions:

- The Gospel of Thomas is a coherent, intricately organized book of 131 wisdom poems, not 114 "collected" sayings as scholars have thought. About half of them are more ancient versions of Jesus' parables and sayings in the New Testament.

- Jesus probably *composed* the Gospel of Thomas. It is unlikely that anyone other than Jesus could have understood his sayings and parables so well that he could intricately organize them into a coherent Book.

- The Gospel of Thomas chapters are in the form of a Semitic literary style called a "chiasm" or "arch." You read the first chapter, then the last parallel chapter, then the second, and then the second from the last, and so on. The main concept is in the keystone (center) Chapter Eleven.

- When this new knowledge of Semitic signals is applied to the books of the Bible, it discloses the true organization of these books. They contain major and minor divisions, and within them, a type of Semitic poetry, not the columns of prose we read today.

- The newly discovered Semitic signals tell us how to read the text to understand the meaning of metaphors and passages. Most of the words and phrases such as "ark," "wilderness," and "walking on the sea" are primarily metaphors and not physical objects and actions. Further, many of the books should be read as pure allegories, or allegories that rely loosely on some historical information. They are not pure histories.

- The organization of most Biblical books and passages tell us how to understand the author's *embedded* dictionary and commentary. Thus, we have less need for external dictionaries and commentaries, and we can check the basis of current theology and interpretations.

- The organization of most Biblical books and passages is so tight that it betrays when a later copyist deleted or added text. Thus, we can correct ancient manuscripts.

- The Gospel of Thomas *combined* with Jesus' sayings in the New Testament fully explains his revolutionary, hitherto seemingly unknown, shocking "gospel" (Mk 1:14), "way" (Acts 9:2), and method for knowing the "will of God" (Mk 3:35). I call Jesus' approach, his "Way of the Soul." Its three major principles that he discovered through direct observation of his experience of people and nature:

    1. We were born saved, innocent, pure, perfect, one with ourselves, others, plants, and animals; and *full* of the life of God.

2. We became "divided" from our real selves and from our brothers and sisters when we allowed adults to convince us that we were "good" when we blindly believed their religious and social dogma and "bad" when we did not. Jesus calls this way of thinking, psychological "death."

3. We become "one" again with ourselves, everyone and everything by making the ideas of authorities (clerics, parents, politicians, peers, professors, authors of scriptures, therapists, etc.) *secondary* to listening to our common soul-Voice which will guide us unerringly to peace and fulfillment. When we do that, we become more fully "alive" by returning to being an all-loving child, but with the wisdom to guard ourselves from people who want us to be what we are not.

- Jesus' Way of the Soul is an expansion of Abraham's Covenant. Jesus criticized the Way of Moses, and by extension, all dogma-indoctrinating religions and institutions, which are what I call, the "Way of the Mind." Neither Jesus nor Abraham established a dogma-indoctrinating religion. Instead, they taught people to listen to and live from their soul-Voice. Their goal was to empower people to make their own decisions, not to control how they thought and acted.

- Jesus' revolutionary message is one that people attached to dogma-indoctrinating religion, to tradition, and to religious and secular authoritarian control would find not only hard to live but to be a deep personal and social threat. That would explain what motivated religious and secular authorities to murder him, why his followers hid Thomas, why they established many conflicting communities each with their own convenient interpretation of his message, why Paul the Apostle never quoted him, and why the Nicene Creed contains no statements from Jesus' parables and core sayings. As a result, most people today do not understand that dogma-indoctrinating Christianity is not the true gospel of Jesus.

- There are two forms of most religions: one part that is dogma-based, and the other, that makes soul-knowing primary. We often call the first "organized religion" and the second, "mystical religion." Jesus expanded upon and concretely systematized the latter. He was critical of the former.

SUMMARY

Jesus was a therapist, not a theologian, cleric, or nationalistic zealot. In Thomas, he lays out a theory of personal development that is a universal "Way" for everyone—including Atheists. Therefore, he was the Messiah who proclaimed the paradigm-shift solution for personal and world peace that we need today.

THIS STANDARD EDITION OF THE GOSPEL

You, the reader, will discover the following in this book you are reading now:

1. The story of the discovery of the Gospel of Thomas;

2. The entire Gospel it is original poetic arrangement;

3. Evidence that Jesus composed the Gospel of Thomas;

4. Evidence that Jesus was the Messiah with the message that could unify humankind and bring about an era of unprecedented world peace;

5. A Primer for those desiring to begin immediately practicing Jesus' Way of the Soul is in Appendices Ten and Eleven. Some may want to read this Primer before reading the main book.

6. An Overview of Jesus' Unknown Revolutionary gospel,

7. A Self-Examination that enables the reorder to measure his progress on Jesus' "Way"

A Companion Book:

Another Book explains in detail Jesus' Way of the Soul and contrasts it with Paul the Apostle's reformulation of Jesus' gospel into his Way of the Mind.

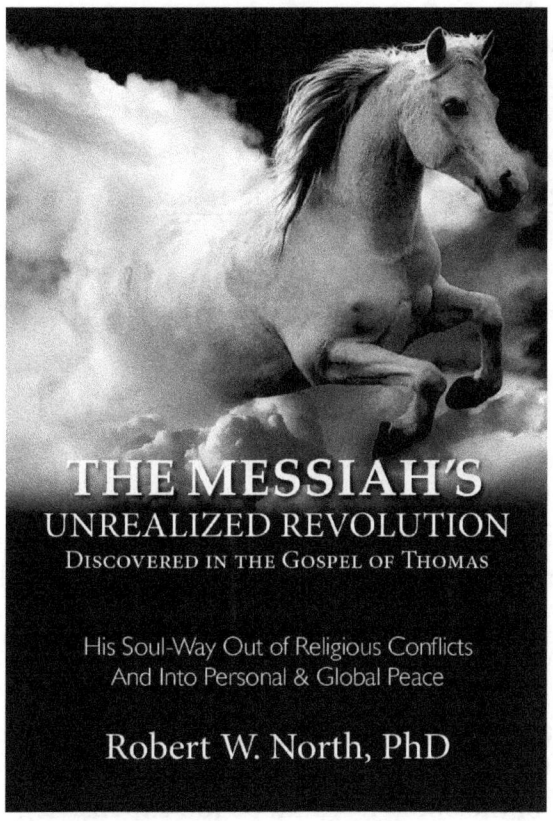

In "The Messiah's Unrealized Revolution," you will find:

1. 53 of Jesus' wisdom poems, explained from the full Gospel of 129 poems. I selected those poems and organized them so that they explain the main elements of his theory of personal development,

2. A comparison of Jesus' message with that of the Apostle Paul, which forms the basis of Christian theology,

3. An Overview of Jesus' Unknown Revolutionary gospel,

4. A Primer for living Jesus' Gospel, and

5. A Self-Examination that enables the reorder to measure his progress on Jesus' "Way,"

6. Evidence that Jesus was the Messiah with a message that, if lived, will bring unity to the world fractured by religious conflict, and

7. Evidence that Jesus composed the Gospel of Thomas.

ADDITIONAL MATERIALS

- The digital version for electronic reading devices, tablets, phones and computers can be purchased at **www.7771.org**.

- The companion books and forthcoming training materials can also be examined at **www.7771.org**.

- You may also register your interests at that site. We will be establishing forums for people to connect with others on Jesus' Way, offering free video and other guides and providing a bookstore for other authors who teach his Way.

- I and my colleagues welcome any feedback. If you wish, please contact us at **www.7771.org**.

ABOUT ROBERT NORTH

Robert North was a former member of the Society of Jesus (Jesuits). There he was educated in the classics, history, the humanities, and philosophy. After he left that order of priests and brothers, he earned a Ph.D. in Counseling at the University of Florida. While working in several colleges and universities, he continued the scripture scholarship that he began as a Jesuit. His focus has been on discovering the Semitic Principles used by the authors of the *Bible* and the *Gospel of Thomas* to organize their works.

(You will notice below that the book skips to page 37. The reason: early readers asked for the material on pages 7 to 36 be put later in the book. We did that; however, we did not repaginate because of the complexity of the book. It would be too expensive.)

PRELIMINARY

THE DISCOVERY OF THE GOSPEL OF THOMAS

The Gospel of Thomas and the New Testament?

For more than 300 years after Jesus died, those who revered him argued about what to include in a New Testament. They could not agree because they each wanted texts that supported their own doctrines. In the 4th century, the leaders of the Church of Peter and Paul (which today is known as the Roman Catholic Church) finally listed the documents we typically find in the New Testament. They were able to make their decision final for others because they had been appointed by Constantine, the Emperor of the Roman Empire to do so.

The Roman Christian Church Bishops based their doctrine on Paul, the Apostle. Logically, those leaders excluded any document antithetical to their creed, such as the Gospel of Thomas. With the backing of Rome, they also ordered both the destruction of all documents with competing doctrines and the persecution of people proclaiming them.[1]

Background

In the mid 1940s, the world became aware of two magnificent archeological discoveries. The first occurred in Egypt in 1945 and is known as the "Nag Hammadi Library." These Books are mostly Christian writings composed in the first three centuries C.E. The second, better known to laypeople, occurred in 1947, and is known as the "Dead Sea Scrolls." The Dead Sea Scrolls are Jewish writings composed before 70 C.E.

The Nag Hammadi Discovery

In December of 1945, in Upper Egypt near the current city of Nag Hammadi (see the map below), two brothers, Muhammad 'Ali and Khalifah, set off on their camels to obtain nitrogen rich soil for use as fertilizer.

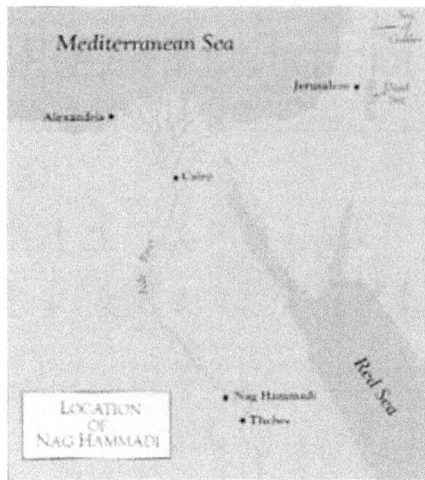

Figure 1. *Nag Hammadi in Egypt*

At a large mound called Djebel el Tarif, the brothers began to dig. Soon Muhammad 'Ali unearthed a large, sealed clay pot. Inside he found thirteen leather bound codices filled with crumbling yellowed parchment.

Figure 2. *Area of the Discovery*

Figure 3. *Muhammad 'Ali Who Led the Expedition*

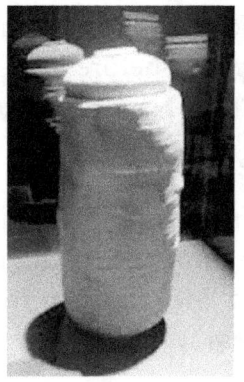

Figure 4. *120 CM High Jar*

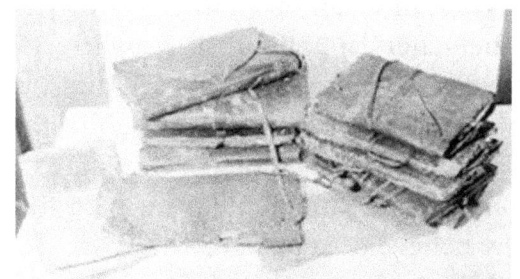

Figure 5. *Thirteen Codices*

Figure 6. *A Single Codex Containing Many Books*

Although he was unable to read the text, Muhammad 'Ali knew that the books were ancient and possibly worth a lot of money if sold to antiquities dealers on the black market in Cairo.

What Muhammad 'Ali had discovered was a collection of books that included many Coptic copies of Christian manuscripts composed before 300 CE. Most of the originals seem to have been written in Greek, the language of the New Testament. The buried manuscripts date from the third and fourth centuries.

Muhammad 'Ali took the books to his house. While he was out on an errand, his mother ripped out some of the pages and began to burn the manuscripts as kindling. Fortunately, before all was destroyed, Muhammad 'Ali hid them from her and from the authorities who would confiscate them. He placed them with different friends.

Those friends began to sell them in Cairo. It didn't take long for the books to come to the attention of the Egyptian Department of Antiquities. Over the course of many years, the books were collected and became the property of the state.

While the Dead Sea Scrolls became famous rather quickly, the Nag Hammadi Library was largely unheard of by the general public until the early 1970s. One of the barriers to publication was the absence of scholars who could read and translate Coptic, the language of the documents. The second reason for the hesitant publication was that scholars initially dismissed the documents as arising out of a branch of Christian thinking, called "Gnosticism." They did not believe that Gnosticism contributed much to our understanding of Jesus or early Christianity. Now, many believe the opposite.[2]

THE GOSPEL OF THOMAS

One of the codices contained a Book that scholars today call the "Gospel of Thomas." They gave it that name because a scribe wrote in the last page of the document, "Gospel of Thomas," as shown below in the middle of the page on the left.

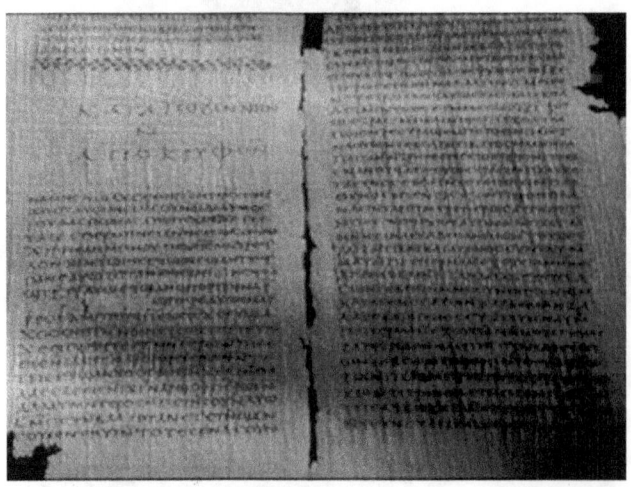

Figure 7. *Two Pages from Coptic Text of the Gospel of Thomas*

The Gospel contains what scholars in the 1950s, shortly after its discovery, considered to be 114 wisdom sayings. In the next volume of this series (*The Gospel of Thomas: The Original 21-Chapter Poetic Arrangement*), I will present evidence that the Gospel contains 129 highly organized poems rather than 114 sayings. The Gospel is so tightly organized that I will argue that only one person could have done it, that person had to have known all of the poems in depth, and that person was probably Jesus.

This "newly discovered" Gospel has become sensational among students of early Christianity. It is studied today not only more than the other Nag Hammadi writings, but also more than any other early Christian document. The reasons are many:

First, Thomas contains, in some form, about 50% of the parables and sayings that are in the Gospels of Mark, Luke, Matthew and John. This drives scholars to attempt to discover whether Thomas was composed before or after the New Testament Gospels, and by whom?[3]

Some scholars who compare the literary style of the Thomas material to that in the New Testament Gospels find the style in Thomas to be more primitive—implying pre-New Testament composition. For example, in Thomas, the Parable of the Sower does not contain an explanation; in Mark, the first New Testament Gospel thought to have become published before 70 C.E., there is an explanation. If these scholars are correct, and the style and content of Thomas are more primitive, then it is possible all or parts of the Gospel of Thomas were together before or shortly after Jesus died.

A second reason Thomas is more studied than the rest of the Nag Hammadi Library is that the content of the Gospel of Thomas expresses emotionally moving, practical wisdom instead of the abstract, blind belief religious theology that is found in many other early Christian texts. Thus, religious and nonreligious people that are interested in personal development may find the content enlightening.

A third reason for the intense interest in Thomas concerns the first sentence in the Gospel of Thomas, in which Jesus is identified as the author, as shown below:

Gospel Prologue

These are
the words,

Those hidden,

Which

Jesus,

Who lives,

Spoke.

It is worth noting that despite the fact that no other early Christian text begins with such a hugely remarkable claim, scholars have generally dismissed the possibility that Jesus composed the Gospel. They cite various reasons:

A Book written by Jesus would have been well known. We possess no historical evidence that Jesus composed a Book before he died. However, if what Jesus wrote was so inflammatory, so revolutionary, and such a threat to secular and religious authorities, that anyone caught with such a Book might be killed, such a Book would have been well hidden for many years.

The Gospel of Thomas was known by that title, and not as the "Gospel of Jesus," as early as the beginning of the third century.[4] However, that title may not mean anything as most early works were not titled as composed by their original authors. For example, we do not know for sure who authored the Gospels in the New Testament. It was common, in the first few centuries C.E., for communities to give their works legitimacy by labeling them as having been written by people with close ties to Jesus.[5]

A fourth reason for the massive interest in the Gospel of Thomas concerns the degree to which its content diverges from current Christian theology. In it, we find no trace of Paul's notions that one is "saved" because he believes

1. in original sin,
2. that Jesus died on the cross to wipe out original sin, and
3. that Jesus was resurrected.

Jesus died in 30 C.E. Paul composed his first letters in about 50 C.E. If Jesus composed all of the material in the Gospel of Thomas, or someone shortly after Jesus collected material and added it to what Jesus composed, we would expect that the Book would not include any references to Paul's theology. That, in fact, is the case. We have no historical record of Jesus believing in original sin or in any of Paul's other core ideas.

A fifth reason that the Gospel of Thomas is fascinating to students of early Christianity is that scholars know that the Evangelists—Mark, Luke, Matthew, and John—were selecting from one or more larger collections of Jesus' compositions. Much is being written about whether the Gospel of Thomas was one of the early sources of information for the Evangelists.[6]

A sixth reason to study Thomas is that it is not a biographical account of Jesus' life; it does not mention his passion and crucifixion, as we would expect that from a Gospel put together after his death. These factors therefore indicate that the Gospel was composed before Jesus died.

Let us remember that the Gospel of Thomas was discovered 1945. The text is in ancient Coptic, a language understood by few scholars at the time of the discovery. It was not until the 1970s that enough people learned Coptic to translate it and begin studying it.

We are clearly in the very early stages of understanding the nature of this magnificent Book.

ENDNOTES

[1] Elaine Pagels, Beyond Belief, the Secret Gospel of Thomas, Random House, 1995.

[2] Marvin W. Meyer, James M. Robinson, The Nag Hammadi Scriptures: The Revised and Updated Translation of Sacred Gnostic Texts Complete in One Volume, 2009, Introduction

[3] Robert E. Van Voorst, Jesus Outside the New Testament: an introduction to the ancient evidence, Grand Rapids: Eerdmans, 2000, pp 187-193.

[4] Meyer, Robinson, Introduction

[5] Paul J. Achtemeier, The Gospel of Mark, The Anchor Bible Dictionary, Doubleday, p. 545.

[6] James D. Tabor, The Jesus Dynasty, The Hidden History of Jesus, His royal Family and the Birth of Christianity, Simon & Schuster, 2006, 259-71.

INTRODUCTION

How to Read this Book

I argue at the end of this book that Jesus composed the Gospel of Thomas. When I tested the book by asking various kinds of readers to give me their reaction, most had problems understanding Jesus' wisdom poems because of two easily solved problems.

First, no one knew that Jesus composed poems. In fact, that is all he composed. All of his sayings and parables are poems in Thomas and in the New Testament.[1] To create one, he studied people and himself. He then took a kilometer of insights and condensed them down to a centimeter length poem. He chose every word carefully. It took time for him to reflect, compose, and edit a poem. He was an author primarily, not a preacher. One should not speed read the poems, but instead slowly and carefully considers each chosen word and line. It might also be helpful to remember that he describes what we often do not notice. Finally, it is helpful to know that he intends to disrupt our current thinking. Thus, at times we can expect to feel defensive. Those emotions, in turn, can lead us to move on without addressing consciously what has been triggered in us.

Second, when people read the poems for the first time, they could not make them relevant to their lives. We are all living what we know. We get up, rush to get ready for the day, live our normal ups and downs, celebrate when we can, and go on day after day generally repeating the same pattern. We may call that normal, healthy living. Jesus calls that way the way of "death" and "darkness." So, to the degree that we live in darkness, to that degree we cannot easily comprehend poems about living a radically different light way. Jesus describes in Thomas two worlds, each with its own inherent logic and rewards.

Third: People approach Jesus' compositions expecting to read a religious text. Consequently, they misinterpret his parables, poems and sayings. In our modern terminology, The Gospel of Thomas is a unified mental health/character development system. It does not separate spiritual development from personal development. You will not find theological blind beliefs, prescribed rituals, or a list of laws. Jesus was criticizing religion, not founding another one.

---

1 I show this in the professional version of The Gospel of Thomas.

We are accustomed to reading long self-help books about a single aspect of mental health. I have one in my library about how to "forgive." Jesus says the essence of that book and more in a couple of poems using fewer than 100 words. He manages that because he uses ancient metaphors that condense a great deal of information into a single word or phrase, and because he designs his poems so carefully. When one understand the meaning of the metaphors and the organization of the poems, and when one becomes vulnerable to ideas that upset his current views, one can gain great wisdom quickly.

To get into Jesus' poems, generally people need to slow down, read a line at a time, suspend all past beliefs about themselves, others, God, and how to obtain a fulfilled life; courageously consider issues Jesus raises that both prevent and promote personal development, and most importantly, primarily soul-listen and not mind-read. Our souls know already the wisdom in these poems. When a person says to himself, "Why, I already know this, but Jesus says it so beautifully," he has read the poem. After mastering the poems, he may say, "I already knew this entire Gospel, but now I can more efficiently grow with this wisdom daily."

Finally, probably you will read this book very differently than any of your previous ones. The 21 Chapters of this *Gospel* are arranged in an arch or chiasm as you can see on the cover and in the Contents above. One begins by reading Chapter 1, then its parallel, Chapter 21. Then one reads Chapter 2 followed by Chapter 20… and so on until one arrives at the main point or thrust of the Gospel in Chapter 11.

Appendices: As one can see in the Contents, this book contains appendices. To understand the Gospel, I suggest that you read to page 71, and then, read Appendix One, and then, return and read a few more chapters, and then read the next Appendix Two. Those latter two appendices have been designed to make Jesus' message pertinent to your life.

If you wish to study Jesus' Gospel with others, register on **www.7771.org**. We will eventually connect you with others in your physical area, or on the web.

Further Information: If you wish to study Jesus' Gospel with others, register on **www.7771.org**. We will eventually connect you with others in your physical area, or on the web.

CHAPTER 1
SAYING 1

Poem 1, Part 2
(1)

And
he
wrote them

Namely,
(inwardly)¹
the twin²
Judas³

(And outwardly)¹
the Twin.⁴

¹*Inwardly:* According to Semitic Parallelism rules, "inwardly" and "outwardly" are implied.

²*The Twin:* the Greek word, "Didymus," meaning, "twin."

³*Judas:* Jesus had two disciples named Judas.

⁴*Twin:* the Aramaic word, "omas," meaning "twin" is used here.

Poem 1, Part 1   ← ↑ →   **Poem 1, Part 3**
(1)   (1)

These
are
the words¹

Those
hidden²

Which
Jesus
(discovered)³

Who
lives⁴

Spoke.

¹*Words:* Wisdom ideas

²*Hidden:* We hide wisdom from emerging from us. We will learn that Jesus thinks we have access to unlimited wisdom. We only need to "reveal" it.

³*Discovered:* Implied. See part 3.

⁴*Lives:* See the note on the next page.

Whoever
(listens to)¹

And
discovers the meaning
of these words²

Will take a taste
not
of death.³

¹*Words in parenthesis are implied in this Book.*

²*Discovers the meaning of these words:* Discovers the meaning for practical living at a higher level of life.

³*Death:* See the note on the next page

- Underlined words designate parallelism. ( ) indicates text that is not in the Coptic text but that is implied. See the Section below for an explanation of this three-part Chapter.

EXPLANATION OF CHAPTER ONE

THE ARCH (CHIASTIC) ARRANGEMENT

Chapter One consists of three parts in an arch. This is a common way to organized material in the ancient Semitic oral culture that created the Bible.

In an arch arrangement, there are three parts: The left side, the upper keystone, and the right side. The right and left side can consist of many units. In Chapter one, there is one unit. The keystone unit is almost always a single unit.

A unit can be a chapter. You see that on the front cover that shows 21 chapters in an arch. Units can be poems. Many of the chapters in Thomas are arranged in an arch of poems. You can see that in the Table of Contents. Units can also be stanzas in a poem, as you will see in this Gospel.

One reads a left side unit first. Then, one reads the parallel unit in the right side. Those two units explain each other. Sometimes they expand upon each other, sometimes one will exemplify the other, sometimes one will complete the other, and sometimes they say the same thing with different words.

Two parallel units are considered to be positively parallel if they essentially agree with each other. That relationship is shown with the symbol: ←→. Two units are negatively parallel when they express opposite ideas. That relationship is shown with the symbol: →←. In Chapter One, Parts 1 and 3 are positively parallel.

In general, the units on the left side express the condition for personal development. The units on the right side explain the result. The keystone explains the action, thinking, or person that uses the condition to transform or not transform himself or the situation. Therefore, the keystone or pivotal unit is the most important unit in the arch. Units on the left side point up to the keystone, and those on the right obtain their meaning from the keystone. When two positively parallel units point to the keystone, you will see the symbol: ←↑→. When two negatively parallel units point to the keystone, you will see the symbol: →↑←.

If the keystone expresses transformation, the right side will often show as a result, an increase in life or development. In Part One, the author tells us that words are hidden within us. In the keystone, Jesus discovers the meaning of those words and their meaning. On the right side we learn that as a result of his transformation, he psychologically/spiritually "lives" and is able to speak the words to others.

(As an aside, the author of Thomas does not distinguish between psychological and spiritual development. He does not even use the word "spiritual." Implied, he tells us that they are the same action.)

(As another aside, in the Professional Edition I provide the evidence that the author of Thomas is Jesus. One important part of that argument states that because of the intricate organization of the Gospel, one would logically conclude that most likely only a single person could have composed it. Because we know from the New Testament Gospels that Jesus authored about half of the content in Thomas, Jesus is the most likely the author).

If Jesus had not discovered the meaning of the hidden words, the right side would have expressed that he psychologically/spiritually died. In Part 3, that is expressed.

In the Keystone poem, Jesus used the word "twin" twice. That tells us that to transform ourselves, we need to become a "twin." We might ask, "a twin of whom?" That is explained in the parallel Chapter 21.

Now, please look at the cover. Notice that the entire Gospel is arranged in an arch of chapters. Then, look at the Table of Contents. You will see that each chapter consists of poems. In many chapters they are arranged in an arch. In the other chapters, they are arranged in two parallel columns, which is another way that the Semites organized material.

The book is arranged so that you will read Chapter One followed by its parallel in Chapter 21. There you will find metaphors or the actual words for the key words in Chapter 1, such as "twin," "hidden" "discover," and "lives." When you read each chapter, you also will read the poems in parallel. The parallel chapters and poems explain each other.

In the Professional Edition, a number of the Appendices explain much more about the arch and column arrangements.

LIFE AND DEATH

By the words "life" and "death," Jesus does not refer to spiritual, intangible events. Rather, he talks about our actual extreme experiences. Each person needs to examine his own life and decide for himself the meaning of "life" and "death."

To do that, think of a time when you are most alive. Then, think of a time when you experienced yourself as *most* "dead." That is what Jesus did. He paid attention to those two extremes and defined them in various ways in this Gospel.

Jesus describes life as the experience of personal and spiritual fulfillment (He does not separate the two). *Life* is also living with great wisdom, being in the moment, and being without a false self to promote or defend. An alive person is a king or queen over himself and his interactions with others. He is one with all. Most importantly, he is love in the face of any person or event no matter how painful or upsetting while guarding himself from the limitations of that other person or the event.

Jesus describes the experience of death as one of unfulfillment, confusion, and mentally and emotionally bouncing between the past and future. To live death is to be "divided" both between one's real and false selves and from others. Today we seek relief from death in distractions, busyness, sex, alcohol, and drugs.

When alive, one lives from his soul in oneness with "He who lives." When dead, one lives from his head which is one the expectations of others.

Jesus' model for aliveness—perfect mental and emotional health, is a person who is both a babe and a lion.

A babe is who he is. He is not seeking fulfillment out there by identifying with doctrine, things, and people. He does not crawl around seeking absolute truths. He does not search for money. He wants to love and be loved; however, without compromising his own integrity. He wants to find his own answers, not those of others. Thus, he follows his soul-knowing not the directives of is parents.

Later he will learn that he needs to identify with his parents and their wishes to get love (which causes emotional sickness in him); however, initially, he wants to be himself and be loved for who he is.

A babe needs to learn to be a lion who protects his core self from the unwanted influence of others. Because he is not born a lion, he gradually loses his identification with his core self and begins to identify with is parents and their beliefs. That is how he emotionally "dies."

SOUL-KNOWING

In this *Gospel*, one becomes more alive, more a babe and a lion, by utilizing his soul-knowing, which Jesus calls, "listening" with one's "ear" (singular). In other words, one uses what historically has been called third-ear or third-eye knowing. To do that, one follows a five-step process:

1. **Separate** from the influence of others. Physically retreat to a place of stillness, beauty and comfort; or when that is impossible, find a way to shut out the impact of others on yourself.

2. **Still** yourself in in the beginning, in the NOW. Develop meditation or other techniques for becoming yourself in the present without distracting yourself with past or future thoughts and feelings.

3. **Suspend** all beliefs and feelings about what is true. Recognize that to the degree that you are not fully alive, you do not see the truth. As you grow, the truth becomes more apparent. Thus, suspend all previous beliefs, especially about who you are, who others are, who God is, how the universe functions, and the nature of your problems and solutions. In other words, become empty.

4. Survey the ideas that bubble up from your soul. Ignore ideas that you manufacture with your mind.

5. Select the ideas that tell you how to proceed. After watching the insights flow through you, let your soul lead your mind to decide the meaning of what your soul has presented. Then, let your soul lead your mind to decide how you will engage the world. Your soul leads and your mind follows, not the reverse.

This process is one that you have used when being creative. In this Gospel, Jesus teaches people to use it to know oneself, others and the nature of the principles of personal growth. As one does that, he "reveals" his "hidden" wisdom (words) to become more filled with "life." (Jesus' core message of evolving out of "death" to be full of "life" by using third-ear and eye knowing is explained fully using his poems in the accompanying book: *The Second Coming of Eve, Abraham, Buddha, and Jesus.*)

Chapter 21
Sayings: 106, 108-114

Poem 5
(111a)

The heavens [1]
will be rolled up [2]

And
the earth [3]

In your presence
[4] outward;

And
he

Who
lives

He
out of He

Who
lives

Will peer
not on death.

[4] *The heavens will be rolled up, and the earth, in your presence outward:* As we will see in later poems, Jesus view the growth process as one in which we pass through levels (heavens) of knowledge. When we know on the lowest levels, we see only a shadow of truth. On lower levels we are living as "dead" "men." As we give up our beliefs at a lower level, and use soul-knowing to understand a higher level of heaven, we live at that higher level. Gradually, we come to understand reality truly.
Soul-knowing gives us insights that we nourish in our "earth," that is, our reflective consciousness.
To the degree that we live a high level of heavenly knowing, to that degree the "heavens" and "earth" are "rolled up," that is, they find completion in our use of them.

[1] *The heavens*: One's ability to visualize higher levels of life

[2] *Will be rolled up*: Will be destroyed or completed. Jesus refers to Isaiah 35:1-6: "**1** Come near, you nations, and listen; pay attention, you peoples!.. **2** The Lord is angry with all nations; his wrath is on all their armies. He will totally destroy them… **4 the heavens rolled up like a scroll**… **5** My sword has drunk its fill in the heavens; see, it descends in judgment on Edom, the people I have totally destroyed."

[3] *Earth*: Our ability to reflect on ideas that we gather in our heavenly visions.

Poem 4
(110)

← ↑ →

Poem 6
(111b)

<u>Whoever</u>
has found the <u>world</u>

And
he
comes to be
rich²

Let him
abdicate
from the <u>world</u>.

¹*Whoever has found the world:* Whoever has used his soul-knowing to discover his enslavement to outside authorities.
²*Comes to be rich:* Comes to be wise

³*Let him abdicate from the world:* Let him no longer rule in the kingdom of the world.

<u>Whoever</u>
is
the one

Who
discovers himself
on his own¹

The <u>world</u>²
is
worthy of him
not.

¹*Whoever discovers himself on his own:* Whoever leaves indoctrinators (clergy, political leaders, parents, family, peers, etc.) and uses soul-knowing to discover himself on his own.
²*World:* People who do not discover themselves on their own. Insteard, they let authorities tell them how to think and act.

Chapter 21

Poem 3
(109)

← ↑ →

Poem 7
(113)

The <u>kingdom</u>[1]

It
is comparable
to a man

Who
had
he
there
in his field[2]
a treasure[3]

<u>It</u>
<u>hidden</u>[4]

<u>He</u>
<u>not knowing</u>
<u>about it.</u>[5]

And
after his death

He
left it
to his son

And
the son
<u>did</u>
<u>not know</u>
<u>about it.</u>[5]

He
took the field

Which
was
there

[1]*Kingdom:* An alive person who rules wisely over himself and his interactions with the world.

[2]*Field:* Sphere of personal influence. Internally, oneself. Externally, an environment such as a workplace, a family, or neighborhood.

[3]*Treasure:* Source of wisdom.

[4]*It Hidden:* It concealed by his living death.

[5]*Not knowing about it:* Many people do not know that they possess the ability to use their third ears and eyes to disclose information about themselves, others and how the world works. Instead, they rely on indoctrinating authorities to tell them how to think and act.

*His disciples
asked him:*

"The <u>kingdom</u>[1]

It
is coming

It
on which day?"[2]

*Jesus
responded:*

"The <u>kingdom</u>[3]

It
comes
<u>not in watching</u>[4]
<u>inwardly</u>

And
<u>outwardly.</u>

<u>They</u>
<u>will say</u>
<u>not this:</u>

<u>'Behold here</u>

<u>Or</u>
<u>Behold there.'</u>

Rather
the <u>kingdom</u>
of the Father

It
is spreading
<u>upon the earth</u>[5]

And
<u>men</u>[6]
<u>peer</u>
<u>not upon it.</u>[7]

[1]*Kingdom:* For the disciples: Israel after the Messiah drives out the Romans and restores it in the likeness of David's kingdom.

[2]*Day:* A time when the Messiah would cleanse the temple and bring everyone to worship the one true God.

[3]*Kingdom:* An alive, authoritative way to be.

[4]*Watching:* The kingdom will not come because you disciples stand around watching for what you could not recognize.

[5]*Upon the earth:* Upon the reflective consciousness in my real followers.

[6]*Men:* Dead, blind people

[7]*Peer not upon it:* Cannot recognize those alive.

The Gospel Of Thomas

And
he
gave it
away.⁶

And
whoever
bought it⁷

He
came plowing⁸

And
he
discovered the
treasure.⁹

And
from the treasure
he
began to give money
at interest¹⁰

He
to those

Whom
he
desired.

⁶*And gave it away*: He did not know that he had hidden wisdom; so he kept passing on his dead ways to others.

⁷*Bought it*: Paid the price of living in the moment so that he could soul-know his hidden treasure.

⁸*He came plowing*: He reflected on what he soul-sensed. He turned over his new ideas this way and that.

⁹*Discovered the treasure*: the meaning for his life of the wisdom he soul-discovered.

¹⁰*He began to give money at interest*: He began to speak wisdom with the expectation that others use it to become more alive.

Chapter 21

Poem 2
(106)

← ↑ →

Poem 8
(114)

When
you
should <u>make the two
the one</u>[1]

You
will come to be
the sons of man.[2]

And if
you
should say this:

"Mountain[3]
move"

It
will move.[4]

[1]*When you should make the two, the one:* When you should stop being split between your real and false selves, and instead, become a twin of your real self. Also, when you should stop dividing yourself from others, and instead, become their twin.

[2]*Sons of Man:* In Poem 5, Jesus speaks of his followers as "Sons of the Father." In Chapter 15: Poem 5 (3c), he calls his followers sons of "Light." us, the phrase "sons of man" means in some contexts, "sons of the Father" or "sons of Light."

[3]*Mountain:* A person with the characteristics of a mountain: solid, noble, still, awe inspiring, beautiful, indomitable, reaching to the heights, etc.

[4]*Mountain move, and it will move:* An alive person is grand stillness in the world; yet, he can command himself to move.

Simon Peter
said to them
this:

"Make Mary
leave us

For
women
are
worthy not
of life."[1]

Jesus
said this:

"Behold!

I
myself
will lead her[2]

So that
I
might <u>make her
male</u>[3]

So that
she
might come to be
a spirit

She
living
and
<u>resembling
you males.</u>[5]

For
any woman

Who
<u>makes herself
male</u>

Will go
into the kingdom
of the heavens.[6]

[1]*For women are worthy not of life:* For women are not worthy of life in the kingdom.

[2]*Lead her:* Empower her, teach her.

[3]*So that I might make her male:* So that I might show her how to identify with her core life and the identical core life in men, rather than identify with her gender.

[4]*Might come to be a spirit:* Might come to live from He and She who lives.

[5]*She resembling you males:* When we identify with our gender, we take on a false self and stop being "one." Instead, we are "two."

[6]*Will go into the kingdom of the heavens:* A "heaven" is a level of knowing. "Kingdom of the heavens is a high way of ruling over oneself. Those on Jesus' Way pass through heavens as they grow. Those committed to false selves built around a doctrine, things, people, their gender, etc, do not pass through heavens, but instead, devote themselves to defending and promoting their false identities at a low level of growth.

57

The Gospel Of Thomas

Poem 1
(108)

Poem 9
(This poem is missing in our Coptic text. It is the last poem in the book, and was probably torn off. Six other chapters end with this "ear" poem; so we can guess that this chapter ends with it. It is also a perfect parallel to Poem 1)

Whoever
<u>drinks</u> out
of my mouth¹

Will come to be
in my way²

And also
I
myself

Will come to be

As
he
is.³

And
those things⁴

Which
are
hidden⁵

Will appear
to him.

¹*Whoever drinks out of my mouth*: Whoever listens to me and nourishes himself with my wisdom.

²*Will come to be in my way*: Will evolve in wisdom and life as I have done. (Jesus states that he was not born perfect, but developed himself just like we must to be fulfilled.)

³*Will come to be as he is*: Will share the same life

⁴*Those things*: Those words, insights, concepts.

⁵*Which are hidden*: Which he hides from himself.

He

Who

has

his ear¹

to <u>listen</u>

Let him
<u>listen</u>.

¹*Ear*: Third ear. When one uses his third ear and/or eye, he soul-senses information. It passes through him from another source. Otherwise, we are using two ears and eyes. One ear and eye is focused on the expectations of others, and the other on our inner voice. That is the cause of anxiety, worry, and inner division. We become healed when we choose to live in the moment, sensing with our soul the information we need to take the next step. Our soul one with all knows all. It knows nothing happens by accident, and how to proceed with exactly what is going on.

Chapter 2
Saying 2-8

Poem 5
(3b)

When
you
should know yourselves [1]

Then
they
will know you [2]

And
you
will realize

That
you
are
sons
of the Father [3]

Who
lives.

If
you
will know yourselves
not

Then
you
exist
in poverty [4]

And
you
are
the poverty. [5]

[1] *When you should know yourselves*: When you should give up your current precious beliefs about yourselves and soul-know who you really are at a higher level.

[2] *Then, they will know you*: All will notice that you walk, talk, and make decisions from "He who lives within."

[3] *You are sons of the Father*: You are sons and daughters of God, exactly like Jesus. Jesus does not say that he is not the son of God, rather, that at our core, we all are. We need to reveal that truth to ourselves by knowing ourselves.

[4] *You exist in poverty*: You exist without wisdom.

[5] *You are the poverty*: You contribute to the confusion and death in the world.

Poem 4
(5)

Know he [1]

Who
is
in the presence
of your face [2]

And
he

Who
is
hidden
from you [3]

He
will be <u>revealed</u>
to you. [4]

<u>For nothing</u>

It
<u>hidden</u>

That
<u>it</u>
<u>will appear outwardly</u>
<u>not.</u> [5]

[1] *Know he*: Soul-know in depth another.

[2] *Who is in the presence of our face*: Who is there, but to whom you do not pay attention.

[3] *Who is hidden from you*. Others are always hidden from us to some extent.

[4] *He will be revealed to you*: His true and false selves will be revealed to you.

[5] *For nothing, hidden, that it will appear outwardly not*: We have infinite wisdom if we use soul-knowing to access it. We do not need indoctrinators. On a deserted island, we can grow in wisdom.

Poem 6
(6)

Part 1

Jesus' disciples asked him:

"Do
you
want

That
we
fast?

And
what
is
the manner

That
we
will pray?

And
shall we
abstain
from certain foods?"

And
shall we
give alms? [1]

Part 2

Jesus responded:

"You
do
not speak lies [2]

And
what
you
hate in him

→← **Part 1**

[1] In all of those questions, the disciples want Jesus to indoctrinate them. They are not soul-seeking. They do not want to live from their inner voice, but rather from external laws.

[2] *Do not speak lies*: Do not be what you are not if you expect to reveal to yourselves who others truly are.

Chapter 2

Part 2
← ↑ →

You
do
not do
to him; ³

For
they
are <u>revealed</u>

<u>All of them</u>

In the presence
of heaven." ⁴

³ *What you hate in him, do not do to him*: What we hate in others ultimately is dishonesty

⁴ *They are revealed …in the presence of heaven*: Others are shown to us for what they are when we are "heaven," that is, our highest, alive, honest self; not when we are our false selves.

Poem 3
(4)

← ↑ →

Poem 7
(7)

He
will delay
not

Namely
the man
of maturity
in his days ¹

To <u>ask</u> a little
small <u>child</u>

He
being
of seven days ²

About the place
of life. ³

And
he
will live. ⁴

¹ *The man of maturity in his days*: The person who has grown in enlightened wisdom.

² *Seven*: Biblically, "seven" symbolizes "perfection." The child is born perfect; he has not been corrupted by the world. He has no original sin.

³ *Place of life*: That place within, from which we think and act full of life.

⁴ *He will live*: He will model himself after the child.

<u>A blest one</u> ¹

He
is
the <u>lion</u> ²

The <u>one</u>

That
the man ³
will <u>eat</u> ⁴

And
the <u>lion</u>
comes to be
the man ⁵

And
he
is cursed ⁶

Namely
the man ⁷

¹ *A Blessed one*: A person chosen by God.

² *Lion*: A person who guards his aliveness, his inner child.

³ *Man*: A seeker of the life and wisdom of the lion.

⁴ *Eat*: Takes in the wisdom of the lion, digests it, and makes it part of his life.

⁵ *And the Lion comes to be the man*: And the wisdom and life of the lion comes to be the wisdom and life of the seeker.

⁶ *He is cursed*: He is not favored by God.

⁷ *Man*: A dead person who choses not to learn from the lion.

For
there
are
many first⁵

Who
will come to be
last⁶

And
they
will come to be
single ones.⁷

⁵*There are many first:* There are many wise people.

⁶*Who will come to be last:* Who will seek to learn from those who others regard as "last," such a little child.

⁷*Single ones:* Congruent ones. A little, small child is congruent with his true nature.

The one

That
the lion
will eat⁸

And
the lion
comes to be
the man.⁹

⁸*That the lion will eat:* The lion sees the death in a man and destroys him with a word or glance.

⁹*And the lion comes to be the man:* The man becomes haunted by the memory of a person-lion who is so powerful, wise, and vigilant.

Poem 2
(3a)

Part 1

*If
they
should say to you¹
this:*

"Behold!

The kingdom
is in heaven"²

Then
the birds
of heaven
will come to be
first
before you.³

¹*If they should say to you:* If one in authority should indoctrinate you.

²*The kingdom is in heaven:* Your fulfilled way of being is in "my" heavenly intellectual ideas.

³*Then the birds of heaven will come to be first before you.* Then you will worship the heavenly, intellectual beliefs of the indoctrinator as false gods. (Recalling "Do not put false gods before you"). Exodus 20:3

Part
1
→←
In
oppo-
sition

Poem 8
(8a)

A man
is comparable
to a fisherman
wise¹

The one

Who
threw his net
into the sea.²

And
he
conveyed it up
from the sea

It
full of fish³

Little ones
from below

And
among them

He
discovered a great fish.⁴

¹*Fisherman wise:* A person who seeks his own answers rather than worships the blind beliefs of an indoctrinator.

²*Threw his net into the sea:* Turned his attention to the emotional ideas welling up from his being

³*Fish:* Felt ideas

⁴*Great fish:* A core felt idea that gave him the insight he needed to evolve in life and wisdom.

Part 2

If
they
should say to you
this:

Behold!

The kingdom
is
in the sea" ⁴

Then
the fish
will come to be
first
before you. ⁵

Part 3

Rather
the kingdom

It
is
of your eye
inward

And
it
is
of your eye
outward. ⁶

⁴ *The kingdom is in the sea*: Your fulfilled way of being is in my emotional ideas. "Sea" = "emotions."

⁵ *Then the fish will come to be first before you*. Then, his emotional ideas will be worshipped by you.

⁶ *The kingdom is of your eye inward…outward*: You fulfilled way of being is third-eye-known wisdom about yourself, others and the world.

← **Part 2** →↑←

Part 3 ←↑→

The good man

Namely
the fisherman
wise
threw the little ones

All of those fish

Back down
into the sea ⁵

And
he
chose the great fish
without trouble.⁶

⁵ *Threw the little ones… into the sea*: Discarded the small insights.

⁶ *Chose the great fish without trouble*: The seeker did not shy away from an idea that confronted his inadequacies and give him a vision of how he might evolve.

Poem 1
(2)

Let not
him
stop[1]

Namely
he

Who
<u>seeks</u>

As
he
<u>seeks</u>

Until
he
finds.[2]

And
when
he
should find[3]

He
will be
troubled.[4]

And if
he
should be
troubled[5]

He
will marvel.[6]

And
marveling

He
will come to
reign
over all.[7]

[1] *Let not him stop:* Let not him stop seeking a higher level of life and wisdom.

[2] *Finds:* Finds what he most deeply wants. For example, our minds may want a million dollars yesterday; while our souls want us to be fulfilled at a higher level of wisdom and life.

[3] *He should find:* He should find an insight or vision showing him how he is living a lower level of life and wisdom.

[4] *When he should find, he will be troubled:* When he should find the reason for his lack of fulfillment in life and wisdom.

[5] *And if he should be troubled:* And if he works through his trouble to resolution at a higher level of self and other knowing.

[6] *He will marvel:* He will come to see everything in a new, wonderful, more alive way.

[7] *And marveling, he will come to reign:* He will gain the wisdom to rule over himself and his interactions with others in a more enlightened manner.

←↑→

Poem 9
(8b)

He

Who
has his ear
to <u>listen</u>

Let
him
<u>listen</u>.

Chapter 2

    And
  reigning

     He
will come to be
 in stillness
  with all.

CHAPTER 20
Saying: 100-105, 107, 112

Poem 4
(103)

←↑→

Poem 5
(104)

A blest one
is
the man

The one

Who
knows how
the thieves[1]
will come in;

So that
he
may rise[2]

And
he
gather his kingdom[3]

And
he
bind himself
upon his loins[4]
from the beginning[5]

Before
they
come in.[6]

[1]*Thieves:* Those indoctrinators who seduce the alive into dying conformity.

[2]*Rise:* Become soulaware of himself

[3]*Gather his kingdom:* Gather his knowledge of himself, others and the world.

[4]*Bind himself upon his loins:* Become powerfully determined.

[5]*From the beginning:* From the stillness of being in the present, in the "now."

[6]*Before they come in:* Before they lead him astray

They
said to Jesus:

"Come[1]

And
pray[2]
today

And
fast."[3]

Jesus
responded:

"For
what
is
the sin[4]

That
I
have done

Or
how have
I
been defeated?[5]

Rather
when
the bridegroom
comes out
of the bridal-chamber[6]
Then
let them
fast

And
let them
pray."[7]

[1]*Come:* Leave your Way of living

[2]*Pray:* Do a religious ritual that is necessary to get God to help you.

[3]*Fast:* Do another religious ritual in order to be clean and worthy of God's assistance.

[4]*Sin:* An offence against God

[5]*How have I been defeated:* From the Parallel Poem 4: How have I been defeated by a "thief"

[6]*When the bridegroom comes out of the bridal chamber:* When I finish my time of intimate communication with my Parents, and get the inspiration for how to proceed,

[7]*Let them pray:* let the thieves watch out; for, I am a lion guarding and attacking.

The Gospel Of Thomas

Poem 3
(102)

Woe to them the Pharisees [1]

For they resemble a dog [2]

He resting [3] upon the manger [4] of some oxen. [5]

For resting there

He eats [6] not

And he permits not the oxen to eat. [7]

[1] *Pharisees*: Those who indoctrinate rather than empower people to discover their own hidden wisdom.

[2] *Dog*: The lowest of the low in character. Dogs eat in the garbage dumps.

[3] *Resting*: Not laboring to soul-know.
[4] *Manger*: Place where people go to get their food, that is, their wisdom.

[5] *Oxen*: Stubborn people.

[6] *Eats*: Takes in and integrates what he hears.

[7] *He eats not and he permits not the oxen to eat*: The indoctrinating authorities do not soul-know wisdom, nor do they permit people to use soul knowing to discover their own answers on their own.

Poem 6
(112)

Woe on the flesh [1]

The one

That depends on one's soul; [2] [3]

Woe on the soul

The one

That depends on the flesh. [4]

[1] *Flesh*: False selves in oneself

[2] *Soul*: A unique spirit in a body

[3] *Woe on the flesh...that depends on one's soul*: Oh, the suffering of the false selves that needs the cooperation of the real self. They will forever be in conflict. We experience that when we feel tension, anxiety and worry.

[4] *Woe on the soul...that depends on the flesh*. Oh, the suffering of the real self that has become dependent on false selves.

Chapter 20

Poem 2
(101)

⟷

Poem 7
(105)

Whoever
hates his father
and
his mother
in my way
not [1]

He
can come to be
a disciple
to me
not.

And
whoever
loves his father
not
and
his mother
in my way [2]

He
can come to be
a disciple
to me
not.

For
my mother

She
brought me
forth. [3]

My Mother
however
the true

She
gave to me
life. [4] [5]

[1] *Whoever…way not*: Whoever hates the indoctrination given him by his flesh parents.

[2] *Whoever loves his father… in my way*: Whoever loves his indoctrinating parents, and at the same time, guards himself from their influence

[3] *"My mother, she brought me forth."* My mother, who was living a false life, brought me forth to be like her.

[4] *She gave to me life*: My Mother gave me life that I participate in when I am one with who I am.

[5] Jesus experienced in one God two persons, one he called his "Father," and the other, his "Mother."

He

Who
will know the Father
and
the Mother [1]

He
will be referred to
as
the son
of the harlot. [2]

[1] *He who will know the Father and Mother*: He who will know himself as the life of the Father and Mother; he who will be one with the Father and Mother

[2] *Son of the harlot*: Perhaps equivalent to our saying, "You son of a bitch." We know from the parallel, Poem 2 that the person saying that was upset that Jesus was not living the traditions and religion of his birth mother.

Poem 1
(100)

*They
showed Jesus
a gold piece*

*And
they
said to him*

"Those

Who
belong to Caesar

They
demand of us
taxes." [1]

*Jesus
said to them:*

"Give the things [2]
of Caesar [3]
to Caesar

And
give the things
of God
to God; [4]

And that

<u>Which
is
mine</u> [5]

<u>Give it
to me.</u>

[1] *Taxes*: What one pays for things of common benefit.

[2] *Things*: That which is owed in exchange for common benefits.

[3] *Caesar*: The giver of the common benefits.

[4] *Give the things of God to God*: Return to God your real self with its divine life.

[5] *Which is mine*: Which is owed me for the common benefit. From the parallel Poem 9, we know that that is the lost, rebel sheep.

Poem 8
(107)

The kingdom [1]

It
is comparable
to a man
shepherding [2]

Who
had
he
there
100 sheep. [3]

One
of them
strayed [4]

The greatest
was
he. [5]

He
let go the 99 [6]

And
he
sought after that one

Until
he
discovered it
troubled. [7]

He
said to the one sheep:

'I
<u>desire you</u>

<u>More
than
the 99.</u>

[1] *Kingdom*: An alive way of ruling over oneself and his interactions.

[2] *Man shepherding*: A man who loves and guards all.

[3] *Sheep*: People.

[4] *Strayed*: Became a non-conformist.

[5] *The greatest was he*: He became great because he began to soul-know himself and others on his own.

[6] *99*: Those in the world who identify with their false selves.

[7] *Troubled*: Seekers seek emotional trouble, because it signals something to be released to live more fully. People conform to group-think in order to avoid emotional trouble.

CHAPTER 3
SAYINGS 9-14

Poem 4
(14)

If
you
should fast

You
will beget
to yourselves
a sin;

And
if
you should pray

You
will condemn yourselves;

And
if
you
should give alms

You
will be creating evil
in your spirits.¹

Rather
if
you
should go
into any earth²

And there
you
walk in the districts³

If
they
should receive you⁴

¹Fasting, praying, and giving alms is the way to be righteous on the Way of Dogma and Life. One only needs to be oneself on the Way of Wisdom and Death.

²*If you should go into any earth*: If you should meet any reflective persons.

³*Walk in the districts*: Get to know them in their universe.

⁴*If they should receive you*: If they should embrace you as the life of your Parents

That
which
they
will put in front
of you

Eat it. ⁵

And those

Who
are
sick among them ⁶

Heal them. ⁷

For
that

Which
will go inward
your mouth ⁸

That
will defile you
not.

Rather
that

Which
goes out
from your mouth ⁹

That
will defile you.

⁵ *That which they put in front of you, eat it*. That which they speak, take it in and consider it.

⁶ *Sick*: Those who live the Way of Death

⁷ *Heal them:* Teach them the Way to life and wisdom.

⁸ *That which will go inward your mouth*: The ideas that you take in from others.

⁹ *That which goes outward your mouth*: Those ideas that you speak to others.

Chapter 3

Poem 3
(12)

←↑→

Poem 5
(13)

*The disciples
asked:*

"We
know

That
you
will go
from our hand;[1]

Who
is
he

Who
will come to be
great

He
up over us?"[2]

Jesus replied:

"The place[3]

That
you
will come to[4]
You
will be going up
to James[5]
the righteous;[6]

[1] *From our hand:* From our control.

[2] *He up over us:* He as an authority to tell us how to think and act.

[3] *Place:* The center from which one is himself, in oneness with the life of the Father.

[4] *That you will come to:* at you will be when you stop identifying with your false selves.

[5] *James:* The brother of Jesus

[6] *Righteous:* On Jesus' Way a "righteous" person lives the laws within his being that tell him how to be more alive and wise.

*Jesus
asked his disciples:*

"Compare me[1]

And
you
speak to me
this:

I
resemble
whom?"

*Said
he
to him

Namely
Simon Peter
this:*

"You
resemble
an angel[2]

One

Who
is
righteous.[3]

*Said
he
to him

Namely
Matthew
this:*

[1] *Compare me:* Compare me with others

[2] *Angel:* One who gives us inspiration

[3] *Righteous:* One living according to religious laws.

The one

That
heaven and earth[7]
has come to be
to create him."

[7]*Heaven and earth has come to be because of him:* "Heaven" is our ability to visualize at ever higher levels. "Earth" is our ability to reect. Both are needed for transformation to more life.

"You
resemble
a philosopher

One

Who
is
wise."[4]

Said
he
to him

Namely
Thomas
this:

"Master[5]

My entire mouth[6]
permits me
not to say:

Whom
you
resemble."

Jesus
said to Thomas:

"I
am
your master
not.[7]

Because
you
drank[8]

You
got drunk[9]
from the spring[10]

[4]*One who is wise:* Double meaning: Wise to the ways of the world, or wise on the Way of Wisdom. Matthew probably meant the latter, because Peter clearly does not see the alive essence of Jesus.

[5]*Master:* A person who tells another how to think and act.

[6]*Mouth:* One's ability to express oneself.

[7]*I am Your master not:* "I do not intend to tell you or anyone how to think and act

[8]*Drank:* Soul-listened.

[9]*You got drunk:* You began to stupidly adore me as a controlling leader

[10]*Spring:* Life inspiration

Chapter 3

Which
bubbles; ¹¹

The one

That
I
have measured out." ¹²

And
Jesus
took him ¹³

Withdrew ¹⁴

And
spoke to him
three words. ¹⁵

When however
Thomas
came up
to his companions ¹⁶

They
asked him:

"Jesus
spoke what
to you?"

Thomas said:

"If
I
should speak
to you
one of his words
That
he
has spoken
to me

You
will take stones ¹⁶

¹¹ *Bubbles*: Arises spontaneously within you.

¹² *That I have measured out*: Jesus soul-listened to "hidden" "words" and used his mind to shape the message.

¹³ *Took him*: Chose him

¹⁴ *Withdrew*: Jesus removed him from his worldly death situation.

¹⁵ *Spoke to him three words*: The number "three" symbolizes "transformation."

¹⁶ *Companions*: Companions on the Way of Death.

¹⁶ *Stones*: Strong words.

75

And
throw them
at me." ¹⁷

¹⁷ *Throw stones*: In this context, to confront or attack with words

And
a fire ¹⁸
will come out
from the stones

¹⁸ *Fire:* Passionate meaning embodied by the words

And
it
will burn you." ¹⁹

¹⁹ *Burn you*: Confront you in a way that causes you emotional upset

Chapter 3

Poem 2
(11a)

← ↑ →

Poem 6
(11b)

This heaven[1]

It
will pass away;[2]

And
the one
above it

It
will pass away.[3]

And
those

Who
are
dead

They
live
not.[4]

And
those

Who
live

They
will die
not.[5]

[1] *Heaven:* A level of knowing the truth about oneself, others and the world.

[2] *Pass away:* Our present view of what is true will change as we become more alive. Thus, what we call "true" changes as we grow. (See Appendix 6)

[3] *And the one above it, it will pass away.* As we grow, each level of knowing passes away. for those who are dead, they remain on the same level or devolve to a lower level.

[4] *Those who are dead, live not:* Those who do not seek to grow in knowing truth and life at a higher level, are dead. To live is to "pass" though levels of "heaven."

[5] *Those who live, they will die not:* We cannot live and die at the same time. So, those alive will continue living as long as they continue to evolve.

On the days[1]

That
you
were eating he

Who
is
dead[2]

You
were making him
he

Who
lives.[3]

When
you
should come to be
in the light[4]

What
is
it

That
you
will do to him?[5]

On the days

That
you
were
one[6]

You
made him
two.[7]

[1] *On the days:* At the time when you were clear and open.

[2] *Eating he who is dead:* Listening to and integrating words spoken by a person living a low heaven (level) of truth. E.g. A child who listens and integrates the religious doctrine of his parents.

[3] *You were making him he who lives:* You thought that he was speaking a high heaven (level) of truth.

[4] *When you should come to be in the light:* When you should come to be God-inspired.

[5] *What will you do to him:* Will you see him as dead or alive?

[6] *Were one:* United with your core, true, life. E.g. As a child

[7] *You made him two:* You did not see that he was one also.

When however
you
should come to be
two ⁸

⁸ *Come to be ....two*: When you are two-faced dead.

What
is
it

That
you
will do
to him? ⁹

⁹ *What is it that you will do to him*: Will you be able to see his beautiful, core self? (Implied answer: of course not unless you become one again.)

Poem 1
(9)

←↑→

Poem 7
(10)

Behold! ¹

¹ *Behold:* Soul-see! or third-eye see

He
went out

Namely
he

The one

Who
sows. ²

² *The one who sows:* The one who provides seeds of wisdom (as Jesus does in these poems).

And
he
filled his hand ³ ⁴
(with seed)

³ *Hand:* The ability to control.

⁴ *Filled his hand:* From all of his ideas, he carefully chose his words.

And
he
threw them. ⁵

⁵ *Threw them:* Confronted others with them.

I
have thrown fire ¹
upon the world ²

¹ *I have thrown:* I have confronted people with powerful, upsetting wisdom

And
behold!

² *World:* People who do not listen to wisdom and evolve to a higher level of heaven.

I
watch over it ³

³ *I watch over it:* I make sure it is heard

Until
it
burns. ⁴

⁴ *Until it burns:* Until it makes people uncomfortable

Chapter 3

    And
    some
    were
    indeed
    discovered
on the way. [6]

[6] *Some were discovered on the way*: Some seeds of wisdom were heard by a person on the Way to higher levels of life.

    And
    they
    came

   Namely
the birds [7]

[7] *They came, namely the birds*: The old blind-beliefs of the person came forward in the person's mind.

    And
    they
gathered them. [8]

[8] *Gathered them*: The listener made his blind-beliefs more important than the wisdom.

    And
  some others
   indeed

Were discovered
  on rock. [9]

[9] *Rock*: A closed, stubborn mind.

    And
    they
    did
  not send roots
down to the earth [10]

[10] *They did not send roots down to the earth*: The wisdom did not enter into reflective consciousness.

    And
    they
    did
  not send ears
rising to heaven. [11]

[11] *Did not send ears rising to heaven*: Did not begin listening at a high level of knowing truth.

    And
  some others
   indeed
were discovered
 in thorns [12]

[12] *Thorns*: The wisdom was heard by one with many attachments (for example, to his money, things, family, race, beliefs).

And
they
chocked the seed [13]

And
the worm [14]
ate them.

And
some others
were discovered
in the earth [15]

Which
was
good to them [16]

And
they
gave fruit
up to heaven [17]

Which
was
good to it. [18]

And
it
came

Some
60 per measure [19]

And some
120 per measure. [20]

[13] *Chocked the seed*: The attachments did not give him the freedom to consider the wisdom.

[14] *Worm*: Worry

[15] *Earth*: Reflective consciousness

[16] *Which was good to them*: Which considered them thoughtfully

[17] *Gave fruit up to heaven*: The person became more alive at a higher level of knowing truth.

[18] *Good to it*: The more wisdom we attain, the more that is given to us.

[19] *60 per measure*: A great impact on the inner life of the person who listened and grew. ("Inner" is implied by the arrangement).

[20] *120 per measure*: A very great impact externally on the world. ("externally" is implied).

CHAPTER 19
SAYINGS: 96-99

Poem 3
(96b)

The disciples
said to him:

"Your brothers
and
your mother¹

They
are standing there²

They
on the side
outward."³

He
said to them:

"Those

Who
are
in these places

Who
do the will
of my Father⁴

They
are
my brothers
and
my mother;⁵

They
are
the ones

Who
will go
into the kingdom
of my Father."⁵

¹*Brothers and Mother:* Family indoctrinators.

²*Standing there:* A family can strongly demand conformity to family conventions.

³*On the side outward:* On the side against one desiring life.

⁴*Those who are in those places who do the will of my Father:* Those who live from the center of life with the Father

⁵*They are my brothers and mother:* They are my heart family—they live real life.

⁵*Who will go into the kingdom of the Father:* Who will rule over their real selves as does my Father.

The Gospel Of Thomas

Poem 2
(98)

← ↑ →

Poem 4
(99)

<u>The kingdom of the Father</u>

It
is comparable
to a woman

She
bearing a jar[1]

It
full of meal[2]

She
walking on a way[3]

It
faraway.[4]

The ear[5]
of the jar
broke

And
the meal
emptied out[6]
after her
along the way

And
she
knew
not what
was happening[7]

And
she
did
not realize any
trouble.[8]

[1]*Jar:* Ego, false self

[2]*Meal:* False identities that have nourished her

[3]*Way:* Way of Wisdom and Life

[4]*Faraway:* A long growth journey

[5]*Ear:* Her ear for listening to the world and making important what it says.

[6]*Meal emptied out:* She slowly untangled herself from the allures of the world.

[7]*She knew not what was happening:* She did not control the growth process.

[8]*She did not realize any trouble:* She welcomed "trouble" so much that it was no "trouble." It became an opening for growth.

<u>The kingdom of the Father</u>[1]

It
is comparable
to a man

He
wanting
to kill a man
powerful.[2]

He
drew his sword
in his own <u>house</u>[3]

And
he
stuck it
into the wall[4] [5]

So that
he
might realize

That
his hand[6]
would be
strong.[7]

Then
he
slew the powerful one.

[1]*Kingdom of the Father:* A person listening to the wisdom of the Father who is king over himself and his interactions with others

[2]*He wanting to kill a man powerful:* He wanting to slay his false self.

[3]*He drew his sword in his own house:* He brought up his ideas that divide a true self from a false one in his own being (house)

[4]*Wall:* What separates the true self from a false one.

[5]*Stuck it into the wall:* He attacked one of his false selves.

[6]*Hand:* Ability to control himself:

[7]*That his hand would be strong:* That his inner control would dominate his false self.

Chapter 19

When
she
opened inward
to her <u>house</u>[9]

[9]*Opened inward to her house*: Looked reectively at herself.

She
released the jar
down[10]

[10]*Released the jar down*: Gave up her false self, her ego

And
she
discovered it
empty[11]

[11]*She discovered it empty*: She discovered herself full of life, because her ego was empty

Poem 1
(96a)

←↑→

Poem 5
(96b)

The kingdom
of the Father

<u>It</u>
is comparable
to a woman

Who
<u>took a little bit
of leaven</u>[1]

[1]*Leaven*: Wisdom words

And
she
hid it[2]
in dough[3]

[2]*Hid it*: Protected her insights in herself from those who would not understand.

[3]*Dough*: Reective consciousness

Then
she
made it
into great loaves
of bread.[4]

[4]*Great loaves of bread*: She spoke and became great wisdom in the world for others to eat and digest.

He

Who
has
his ear[1]
to <u>listen</u>[2]

Let him
listen.

[1]*Ear*: Third ear

[2]*Listen*: Soul know wisdom ideas (leaven).

CHAPTER 4
SAYINGS 15-17

Poem 2
(16)

Perhaps
they[1]
are thinking

Namely
men

That
I
have come
to throw peace
upon the world;[2]

And
they
know
not

That
I
have come
to throw divisions
upon the earth:[3]

Fire[4]
sword[5]
and
war.[6]

For
there
are
five[7]

Who
will come to be
in a house[8]

[1] *They:* Dead men and women.

[2] *To throw peace upon the world:* To speak comforting words to those who live death.

[3] *To throw divisions upon the earth:* To divide alive people from dead ones.

[4] *Fire:* Words that confront.

[5] *Sword:* Words that divide them from themselves and others.

[6] *War:* Words that cause a person to fight himself.

[7] *Five:* Five alive and dead people.

[8] *House:* A person. Also a house of people.

There
are
three

Who
will come to be
against two[9]

And
two
will come to be
against three

The father
against the son[10]

And
the son
against the father

And
they
will stand on their feet[11]

They
being
single ones.[12]

[9]*Three against Two:* Three dead people against two alive ones.

[10]*Father against the son:* An alive or dead father against an alive or dead son.

[11]*They will stand on their feet:* Those alive will be powerfully visible and condent in the world

[12]Single Ones: People congruent with themselves.

Chapter 19

Poem 1
(15)

← ↑ →

Poem 3
(17)

When
you
should <u>peer upon</u>
he

<u>Who</u>
<u>was</u>
<u>not begotten</u>
<u>inward</u>
<u>outward of a woman</u>[1]

Prostrate yourselves
onto your face; [2] [3]

And
there
worship him; [4]

He

Who
is
there

He
is
<u>your Father.</u>

[1] *He who was not begotten out of a woman*: When you should see a person with a spirit that a physical woman could not produce

[2] *Face*: Your manifestation of your soul

[3] *Prostrate yourself on your face*: Regard the other with deep respect.

[4] *Worship him*: Venerate the life that he lives

I
will give up
to you
he

<u>Who</u>
<u>did</u>
<u>not</u>
<u>an eye</u>
<u>peer upon him;</u>

And
he

<u>Who</u>
<u>did</u>
<u>not</u>
<u>an ear</u>
<u>listen to him</u>

And
he

<u>Who</u>
<u>did</u>
<u>not</u>
<u>a hand</u>
<u>touch him</u>

And
he

<u>Who</u>
<u>did</u>
<u>not come up</u>
<u>in the heart</u>
<u>of man.</u>

CHAPTER 18
Sayings: 88-95

Poem 4
(91)

←↑→

Poem 5
(92)

They
said to him:

"Tell us! [1]

You
are who

So that
we
might believe
in you?" [2]

Jesus
said to them:

"You
read the face
of the heaven
and
of the earth

And
he [3]
<u>who</u>
<u>was in your presence</u>
<u>outwardly</u>

<u>You</u>
<u>did</u>
<u>not know him.</u>

And
in this moment

You
know
not how
to read him."

[1] *Tell us:* The disciples speak as if they are the "lords" of Jesus.

[2] *So that we might believe in you:* You need to tell us about yourself, because your words and actions tell us nothing. Then, we will decide whether to believe in you.

[3] *He:* My Father and me.

You
seek

And
you
will find.

Yet
those things [1]

About which
you
asked me
in those days

I
did
not <u>tell</u> them
to you

On the day

That
was
there.

Now
it
pleases me
to <u>tell</u> them
to you

<u>And</u>
<u>you</u>
<u>seek</u>
<u>not after them.</u>

[1] *Those things:* Those hidden words of wisdom

The Gospel Of Thomas

Poem 3
(90)

← ↑ →

Poem 6
(93)

Come
up
to me;[1]

For
just
is
my yoke[2]

And
my lordship
is gentle[3]

And
you
will discover a place
of stillness
for yourselves.[4]

[1]*Come up to me:* Leave the dead dogs and seek wisdom and life from me, the one who is a holy pearl. (See poem 6)

[2]*For just is my yoke:* For the work you do to give up your relationship with the dead dogs in return for my wisdom is fair.

[3]*And my lordship is gentle:* I will empower you to find your own answers, not tell you how to think and act.

[4]*You will discover a place of stillness for yourselves:* As one grows, one learns to value stillness more than the company of those dead dogs in the world.

Do
not throw that

Which
is
holy[1]
to the dogs;[2]

So that
they
not throw them
onto the dung heap.

Do
not throw the pearls[2]

Which
are
holy
to the swine;[3]

So that
they
not be made
(into dung).

[1]*Do not throw that which is holy:* Do not wildly disperse your wisdom and your real self

[2]*Dogs:* The lowest of the low.

[2]*Pearls:* You your words of wisdom, so beautiful

[3]*Swine:* Those who are dirty inside.

Chapter 18

Poem 2
(89)

→←

Poem 7
(94)

Why
do
you
wash the side
outward
of the cup? [1] [2]

[1] *Cup*: A person who receives and holds

[2] *Why do you wash the side outward of the cup*: A reference to Jewish purification ceremonies. In other words, why do you wash the outside of a person, when it is inside that he receives the Spirit.

Do
you
understand

That
whoever
created the side
<u>inward</u>

He
is

Also
he

Who
created the side
outward?

Poem meaning: What you are inside will be manifest outside. If you cleaning yourself of false selves inside, you will present yourself as a wondrous, single person outside; however, only those clean of false selves will notice you.

He

Who
seeks

Will find;

And
to he

Who
calls <u>inward</u> [1]

It
will be opened
to him.

[1] *Calls inward*: Who seeks from "He who lives within us"

Poem Meaning: He who "calls inward" creates in himself a cup to receive wisdom.

The Gospel Of Thomas

Poem 1
(88)

The angels [1]
come to you
with the prophets [2]

And
they
will give
to you
those things [3]

Which
you
already have; [4]

And
you

Also
yourselves

Those things

Which
are
of you

You
give them
to others; [5]

And
you
also
say to yourselves:

"On which day
is
it

[1] *Angels*: God's messengers

[2] *Prophets*: People who listened to angles and speak what they heard.

[3] *Things*: Wisdom

[4] *Which you already have*: We reveal hidden wisdom; thus, we do not need prophets.

[5] *Give them to others*: You are like prophets who want something (like adoration) for giving people the inspiration they can receive from angels by themselves.

Poem 8
(95)

If
you
have money [1]

Do
not give it
at interest. [2]

Rather
give it
to he

Whom
you
will take
not
from his hand. [3]

[1] *Money*: Words of value, wisdom

[2] *Do not give it at interest*: Do not give out wisdom to get anything in return

[3] *Rather ... from his hand*: Give wisdom in unconditional love.

Chapter 18

Which
comes

And
they
<u>take</u> he

Who
is
theirs?

CHAPTER 5
Saying 18-19

Poem 2
(18b)

←→

Poem 3
(19a)

A blest one
is
he

Who
will stand on his feet
in the beginning [1]

And
he
will know the end [2]

And
he
will take a taste
not
of death. [3]

[1] *Stand on his feet in the beginning*: To be strong, firm and present in the NOW.

[2] *And he will know the end*: The end is the same as the beginning.

[3] *He will take a taste not of death*: He will not be living in past regret or future worry.

A blessed one
is
he

Who
will come to be
from the beginning [1]

Before
he
comes to be. [2]

[1] *Will come to be from the beginning*: To become present with what is.

[2] *Before he comes to be*: Before he takes the first thought or step to do anything else.

Poem 1
(18a)

The disciples said to Jesus:

"Speak to us
this:

Our end
will come to be
in what manner?" [1]

Jesus
responded:

"For
have
you
revealed yourself
in the beginning [2]

So that
you
will be seeking
after the end? [3]

For
in the place [4]

Where
the beginning
is
there

The end
will come to be
there. [5]

[1] *Our end will come to be in what manner:* The disciples could have been asking about their personal end after following Jesus, or about the end of Jesus's mission, or about the end of times. In all of those cases, they seek their "end" in the *future*.

[2] *Have you revealed yourself in the beginning:* Have you revealed your true self in the present?

[3] *Have you revealed yourself in the beginning; so that you will be seeking after the end:* Have you become you before you begin to proceed; so that you know and are your goal?

[4] *Place:* That part of us from which we think and act.

[5] *For in the place where the beginning is there, the end will come to be there:* For how you begin the journey each second to a fulfilled life is how you will end it.

Poem 4
(19b)

If
you
should come to be
my disciples [1]

And
you
listen
to my words

These stones [2]
will come to be
servants
to you.

For
you
have two trees
in paradise [3]

Which move
not in summer
or in winter [4]

And
their leaves [5]
are not discovered
down.

He

Who
will know them [6]

Will take a taste
not
of death.

[1] *Come to be my disciples:* Come to be in the beginning with me as your end.

[2] *Stones:* Solid words of wisdom

[3] *Two trees in paradise:* The text reads "five trees." Jesus refers to the Garden of Eden Allegory where there are only two trees; so this may be a mistake by a copyist. The two trees are the tree of the knowledge of good and bad and the tree of the knowledge of life. "Paradise" is the Garden and a metaphor for a fulfilled life.

[4] *Which move not in summer or in winter:* Which are still in easy and hard times. A wise person is as joyful and peaceful in hard times as in easy times.

[5] *Their leaves are not discovered down:* Their ideas are of a high way of knowing.

[6] *He who will know them:* He who will be still in the beginning so that he can know with them.

A Core Principle in the Development of Jesus' Way of Life

The previous chapter is one of the foundation principles of Jesus' Way of personal development. He says in 18a:

> Where
> the beginning
> is
> there
> The end
> will come to be
> there.

If we are sorry that we made a mistake, we live in the past. We are not in the present ("in the beginning") one with ourselves. We are what he calls "dead." We are divided from who we are in the NOW.

One who has made a mistake often tries to correct the mistake. In other words, from living in the past and from the past, he tries to make a good life. In other words, from a "place" of death within, he tries to be full of life in the future.

Jesus' insight. One will never be full of life that way. A "place" of death (death thinking) will create more death thinking.

For example, if one invests his money poorly, he may try to correct his mistake by investing wisely. Let us suppose he succeeds in being rich. He was living in the past when he recognized his mistake, he corrects the mistake, but has not learned to live in he present. Thus, he ends up living in the past again. He fears making another mistake no matter how rich he becomes. That is a death cycle.

To begin a life cycle, one needs to follow Jesus' advice in Poem 3.

> A blessed one
> is
> he
> Who
> will come to be
> from the beginning
> Before
> he
> comes to be.

To "come to be from the beginning," one needs to get beyond being "sorry" for a mistake. He needs to be grateful for a mistake. In other words, he needs to be one with it in the present. When he is in the present, he is in the beginning and he is full of life. If instead, he is in the past, he is full of death.

From the "place" of "life," one obtains through soul knowing ideas that lead him to a more fulfilled life as he solves his mistakes. From a "place" of death, one obtains through mental knowing ideas that lead him ultimately to a less fulfilled life as he solves his mistakes.

When we are regretful for the past or worried about the future, we live death. We are not in the "beginning." To get to "the beginning," we need to become still and enable our soul-knowing. From that place in the beginning with soul-knowing, we will always obtain the ideas we need to solve any problem and live a more fulfilled life.

In short: You will not become alive in the present if you begin from past or future dead thinking.

CHAPTER 17
SAYINGS:80-87

Poem 4
(83)

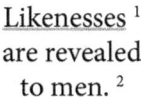

Poem 5
(84)

Likenesses ¹
are revealed
to men. ²

And
the light ³

Which
is in them

Is hidden
in the likeness
of the light
of the Father.⁴

¹ *Likenesses*: The tangible characteristics of the life of the Father and Mother in those alive.

² *Men*: Dead men.

³ *Light*: Singleness, and other tangible characteristics of life

⁴ *The light which is in them is hidden in the likeness of the light of the Father*. The light in an alive person is not seen by those who are dead. They consider darkness, light.

On the days ¹

When
you
look upon your
resemblance ²

You rejoice; ³

When
however
you
should peer upon your
likenesses ⁴

Which
come into being
at your beginning ⁵

And neither
do
they
die ⁶

Nor
do
they
appear outward ⁷

How much
can
you
bear?" ⁸

¹ *Days*: Times of clarity and openness. (Sometimes we are confused and closed).

² *Resemblance*: Your tangible death characteristics, such as living a false self, or being incongruent with your real core self.

³ *You rejoice*: You are proud of your false self.

⁴ *Likenesses*: Tangible characteristics of real life.

⁵ *Which come into being at your beginning*: Which one is only when he is single with his real self in the moment.

⁶ *Neither do they die*: Our real self never dies even if the body dies.

⁷ *Nor do they appear outward*: Do not appear outward to those living death.

⁸ *How much can you bear*: Could you bear to see your potential alive self as a likeness of the Father and Mother.

Poem 3
(82)

He

Who
is
close
to me

Is
close
to the fire; [1]

And
he

Who
is
far
from me

Is
far
from the kingdom.

[1] *Fire*: Hot, wise, confrontive words.

Poem 6
(86)

The foxes [1]

They
have
their dens; [2]

The birds [3]

They
have
their nest; [4]

The son
of man [5]
however

Does
not have a place [6]
to lay his head [7]

Nor
does
he
have
a place
to rest himself. [8]

[1] *Foxes*: Sly, manipulative, dead people.

[2] *Dens*: Places to hide that appear noble, such as state houses.

[3] *Birds*: People of the world who indoctrinate with blind beliefs. E.g. some clergy, parents, professors.

[4] *Nest*: The "nests" of the world are the institutions that both indoctrinate and promote what appears to be good deeds. For example, some churches, temples, and schools.

[5] *Son of man*: A person, such as Jesus, who is full of light (see Ch. 21, Pm. 2)

[6] *Place*: That location within from which we think and act. It can be a "place" of light or darkness.

[7] *A place to lay his head*: A community of like-souled light people who share Jesus' way of thinking.

[8] *A place to rest himself*: A community of like-souled light people who share Jesus' way of acting.

Chapter 17

Poem 2
(81)

Poem 7
(85)

← ↑ →

Whoever has come to be rich[1]

Let him come to be king;[2]

And he

Who has power[3]

Let him abdicate[4]

[1] *Comes to be rich*: Comes to be alive and wise. Comes to be his real self.

[2] *Come to be king*: Come to rule over himself and his interactions with others.

[3] *Power*: The ability to control himself and others. It comes to be out of his wisdom, that is, his ability to understand himself and others.

[4] *He who has power, let him abdicate*: He who is powerful because he rules himself wisely, let him not identify with that wisdom, but with the core life he shares with others.

Adam has came into being out of a great power[1]

And out of a great richness[2]

And he came into being worthy of you not;[3]

For had he been deserving

He would have taken a taste not of death.[4]

[1] *Power*: The wisdom of the Father and Mother.

[2] *Richness*: Fullness of life of the Father and Mother.

[3] *He came...worthy of you not*: Adam was not worthy of a person full of life. He chose to live death.

[4] *He would not have taken a taste of death*. Adam ate the fruit of the tree of the knowledge of good and bad, rather than the fruit of the tree of life. To hide his shame, he covered himself with clothes, which symbolize false selves. That is when he died. The bad fruit is to live in the past and future, in regret and worry. The life fruit is to be in the NOW, in the beginning, in joy.

The Gospel Of Thomas

Poem 1
(80)

← ↑ →

Poem 8
(87)

Whoever
has known the world[1]

[1]*World:* People living death.

Has discovered the <u>body</u>;[2]

[2]*Body:* An inanimate, smelly corpse.

Whoever
however
has discovered the <u>body</u>[3]

The world
is
worthy of him
not.

[3]*Whoever has discovered the body:* Whoever sees the difference between living life and living death in oneself or in another.

A wretched one
is
a <u>body</u>[1]

Which
depends on a <u>body</u>.[1]

And
a wretched one
is
the soul[2]

Which
depends on these two.

[1]*A wretched one is a body which depends on a body:* A suffering one is he who is depends on one or more a false selves. He smells of death.

[2]*A wretched one is the soul which depends on these two:* One suffers when he is torn apart by a battle between his false and real self.

CHAPTER 6
SAYINGS 20-21

Poem 3
(21b)

Let him
come to be
in your midst

Namely
a man
of understanding.[1]

[1]*Man of understanding*: An alive wise person.

Poem 2
(21a)

Mary said to Jesus:

"Your disciples

They
resemble
whom?"

Jesus responded:

"They
resemble
small children
dwelling in a field[1]

Which
is
not theirs.[2]

When
they
should come

← ↑ →

When
the fruit[1]
split open[2]

He[3]
came in a hurry
with his sickle[4]
in his hand[5]

And
he
reaped it.[6]

Poem 4
(21c)

[1]*Fruit*: The characteristics of an -alive person.

[2]*Split Open*: An alive person who is ready to take on the world of the living dead.

[3]*He*: The Father

[4]*Sickle*: A means of dividing the alive person from those dead.

[5]*Hand*: The means of control.

[6]*Reaped it*: Made the alive person manifest in the world of the dead; thus, ultimately upsetting the life of the dead men.

[1]*Field*: An external environment of dead people.

[2]*Children dwelling in a field which is not theirs*: People who are single, one with who they are. They live in environments of dead people.

Namely
the
lords of the field [3]

They
will say this:

'Release our field
back to us.' [4]

And
they
will strip naked [5]
in their presence [6]

So that
it
be given back
to them. [7]

And
it
will be given
back to them." [8]

Therefore
I
speak of it
thus:

"If
he
should realize

Namely
the lord
of the house [9]

[3] *Lords of the field*: Those who want to control the thinking and actions of those alive, the little children. E.g. Some clergy, politicians, parents, professors, peer leaders.

[4] *Release our field back to us*: Conform to our low, dead level of thinking and acting.

[5] *They will strip naked*: The child-adults strip themselves of any pretenses, of any false selves.

[6] They strip naked *In their presence*: The adult-children show that they do not identify with the leaders' ideas.

[7] *So that it be given back to them*: So that those dead can have their level of knowing and deceit.

[8] *And it will be given back to them*: And those demanding to control an environment will choke on their false identities.

[9] *Lord of the house*: An alive leader of his own person.

That
he
is coming

Namely
the robber [10]

He
will keep watch [11]

Before
he
comes;

And
he
will
not permit him
to tunnel
into the house
of his kingdom. [12]

You
therefore
keep watch
from the beginning
of the world; [13]

Bind yourselves
in a great power [14]

So that
not
the thieves
discover the entrance
to the way

To come up
to you; [15]

Because
the help

[10] *Robber*: A manipulative, dominating, indoctrinating leader.

[11] *He will keep watch*: He will use his soul-knowing to see the manipulations of the indoctrinating leader.

[12] *He will not permit him to tunnel into the house of his kingdom*: He will not allow the dead leader to manipulate him into giving up his rule over himself and his interactions with others.

[13] *Keep watch from the beginning of the world*: Guard yourself by being in the moment, which is always the beginning of your world.

[14] *Bind yourselves in a great power*: Develop wisdom

[15] *So that not the thieves discover the entrance to the way to come up to you.* So that the dead manipulators not tempt you into becoming like them.

For which
you
peer outward [16]

It
is
that

Which
will be discovered
in yourselves. [17]

[16] *Because the help for which you peer outward*: Because the insights into false leaders that you seek in the world.

[17] *Which will be discovered in yourselves*: Which will be discovered in yourselves if you use soul-knowing.

Poem 1
(20)

The disciples said to Jesus:

"Speak to us this:

The kingdom of heaven [1] is comparable to whom?"

Jesus responded:

"It
is comparable
to a grain
of mustard [2]

← ↑ →

[1] *Kingdom of heaven*: A person who rules over himself and his interactions because he lives a high level of wisdom and life.

[2] *Grain of mustard*: A person with very tiny soul-known seed of wisdom.

Poem 5
(21d)

He [1]

Who
has
his <u>ear</u>
<u>to listen</u>

Let
him
listen.

[1] *He*: A man of understanding. An alive, wise person.

Chapter 6

"It
smaller

Than
the other seeds [3]

All of them.

When
however

It
should be discovered
in the earth [4]

Which
was worked on [5]

It
sends outward
a great branch [6]

And
It
comes to be
a shelter [7]
for the birds
of heaven." [8]

[3] *It smaller than the other seeds.* A person who possesses wisdom considered small compared to the ideas displayed by dead people.

[4] *When it should be discovered in the earth*: When a person should receive without resistance the inspired insight into his reflective consciousness.

[5] *Which was worked on*: Which was reflected upon.

[6] *Branch*: An ability to hold new wise ideas firmly

[7] *Shelter*: Our place of calm and security from which we live the new wisdom.

[8] *Birds of heaven*: Ideas related to a high level of life or wisdom.

CHAPTER 16
Sayings: 69-79

Poem 6
(73)

⟵→

Poem 7
(74)

The harvest [1]
indeed
is
plentiful;

[1] *Harvest*: Those people seeking life.

O' Lord

There
are
many
around the spring; [1]

[1] *There are many around the spring*: There are many people around their source of inspiration.

The laborers [2]
however
are
few.

[2] *Laborers*: Those empowering people to find their own answers.

Nothing
however
in the well. [2]

[2] *Nothing, however, in the well*: The people do not know how to use inspiration to grow.

Pray
however
to the Lord [3]

So that
he
might send laborers
to the harvest.

[3] *Pray to the Lord*: Be of one mind with the Father and Mother

Poem 5
(72)

A man
said to him:

"Speak
to my brothers

So that
they
might divide the
belongings
of my father
with me."

He [1]
said to him:

"O' man [2]

Who
is
he

Who
has made me
a divider?"[3]

He
turned to his disciples
and said to them:

"Truly

Do
I
exist

I
as
a divider?"

[1] *He*: Jesus

[2] *Man*: Dead man

[3] *Who made me a divider*: Who made me the one to divide a person's real self from his false self."

Poem 8
(75)

There
are
many
standing there
at the door; [1]

Rather
the single ones [2]
are
those

Who
will go into the place
of marriage.[3]

[1] *There are many standing there at the door*: There are many wanting life and wisdom, but not willing to give up being divided between their real and false selves.

[2] *Single Ones*: Those one with their real self.

[3] *Place of marriage*: Oneness with our Parents.

Chapter 16

Poem 4
(71)

⟷

Poem 9
(76)

I
will <u>destroy</u> this house [1] [2]

And
no one
can build it [3]

Never.

[1] *House*: A person. When a "house" has "rooms," the person has false selves. The goal is to have an empty house.

[2] *I will destroy this house*: I will destroy the divisions between my real self and my false selves

[3] *No one can build it*: No one can make me create myself with false selves.

The kingdom
of the Father [1]

It
is comparable
to a man
of trade

Having
he
there
a consignment.[2]

He
discovered a pearl.[3]

The trader

Who
was there [4]

A wise one
was
he;

Therefore
he
gave the consignment
back

And
he
bought
for himself [5]
that pearl
only.[6]

You
also
yourselves

Seek
after his treasure

That
does
not perish

[1] *Kingdom of the Father*: A person who rules over himself and his interactions with others as does the Father.

[2] *Consignment*: All of the things to which one might identify, i.e., wealth, appearance, religion, family, political party, etc.

[3] *Pearl*: Hidden wisdom.

[4] *Who was there*: Who was in the now, in the present, in the beginning

[5] *Bought for himself*: Paid the price of giving up his false selves

[6] *That pearl only*: He gave to dead people those things which are important to them, and he kept the insight leading to living life more fully.

It
enduring in a <u>place</u> ⁷

Where
no moth ⁸
approaches inward
there
to eat

And where
no worms ⁹
<u>destroy</u>
there
anything.¹⁰

⁷ *Place*: Place of life in a person

⁸ *Moth*: Feelings and thoughts that eat away at someone.

⁹ *Worms*: Worry, and fear

¹⁰ *Destroy there anything*: Destroy stillness there

Chapter 16

Poem 3
(70)

← ↑ →

Poem 10
(77)

When
you
should beget
that <u>one</u>[1]
in yourselves

That <u>one</u>

Which
you
have

Will save you.

If
you
do
not have
that one
in yourselves

That one

Which
you
do
not have[2]

Will kill you[3]

[1] *That one:* That alive one, the real self which "lives from He who lives"

[2] *The one which you do not have:* The alive self that you do not have.

[3] *Will kill you:* When we are a false self, we are dead.

I
am
the <u>light</u>[1]

The <u>one</u>

Which
is
upon them[2]

All of them.

I
am
the <u>all</u>.[3]

Has
the <u>all</u>
come outward
of me[4]

And
has
the <u>all</u>
split
to become me.[5]

Split
a timber[6]

And
I
am
there;

Take
the stone[7]
up

And
you
will discover me
there.

[1] *Light:* The likeness of the Father and Mother in the world. The "son of man."

[2] *One that is upon them:* The person who tangibly expresses the life of the Father and Mother.

[3] *I am the all:* I live the life that is in everything, even things that many regard as inanimate

[4] *Has the all come outward of me:* Has the life of our Parents come outward of me.

[5] *Has the all split to become me:* The life of our Parents in all is the same and unique in all. In other words, each alive person possesses the same life, but it expresses itself in each person's unique personality.

[6] *Timber:* A character support in a person.

[7] *Stone:* A word, especially a foundational idea in a person.

Poem 2
(69A)

The blest ones

They
are
those

Who
have persecuted
themselves
in their own heart.[1]

Those

Who
have done that

Have <u>known</u> the Father
in <u>truth</u>.[2][3]

[1] *Persecuted themselves in their own heart*: Confronted their lack of life and sought to be fulfilled.

[2] *Who have done that have known the Father in truth*: Who have known the Father more and more in truth. A person never knows the truth at the highest level of "heaven," of wisdom and life. One is always on the way.

[3] *Known the Father in truth*: Known those with the life of the Father in truth.

⟵→

Poem 11
(78)

Why
did
you
go out to the field?[1]

To see a reed[2]
within
and without
hollow?[3]

And
to see it
moving in
and out
by the wind?[4]

Or
to see a man
in garments[5]
soft[6]
upon him
like
your kings[7]
and
your powerful ones?[8]

Those
in garments
soft
upon them

Can <u>know</u>
the <u>truth</u>
not.[9]

[1] *Field*: Any place where people influence each other.

[2] *Reed*: A person

[3] *A Reed within and without Hollow*: A person empty of false selves, open to being filled with inspired wisdom.

[4] *It moving in and out with the wind*: A person moving about as guided by his inspired soul knowing.

[5] *Garments*: False identities

[6] *Garments soft*: False selves that make a person comfortable with other dead people.

[7] *Kings*: Indoctrinators (Some clergy, politicians, commentators, etc.)

[8] *Powerful ones*: People who use their money and influence to control others.

[9] *Can know the truth not*: They cannot know the truth because they are inherently biased. When we identify with a false self (for example, being wealthy or being a Christian), we automatically distort what we know to protect and promote those false selves.

Chapter 16

Poem 1
(69b)

↔→

Poem 12
(79)

The blest ones

They
are
those

Who
are
hungry [1]

So that
the belly [2]
might be
satisfied [3]

Namely
of he

Who
desires. [4]

[1] *Hungry*: Wanting to take in and digest hidden words of wisdom

[2] *Belly*: One's being

[3] *Satisfied*: Fulfilled with life

[4] *He who desires*: He who desires fulfillment in life

*A woman
in the crowd
said to him:*

"Blessed
is
she
with the belly [2]

Which
bore you;

And blessed
is
she
with breasts

Which
nourished you."

*He
said to her:*

"Blessed
are
they

Who
have listened
to the word
of the Father [3]

And
have protected it
in truth

Some days
will come
into being [4]

[1] *Belly*: Physical womb.

[3] *Blessed are they who have listened*: Birth of life by listening is more important than physical birth and nourishment.

[4] *Some days will come into being*: A person or persons will come into being full of light to confront dead ones in the world.

115

And
you
will say this:

'Blessed
is
she
with a <u>belly</u>

Which
did
not conceive

And
the one
with breasts

Which
did
not give milk." [5]

[5] *Some days… breasts which did not give milk*: The dead are going to be very upset.

Chapter 7
Sayings 22-24

Poem 2
(23)
I
will choose you
one
out of 1,000 ¹
and two
out of 10,000. ²

And
they
will stand on their feet ³

They
being
one ⁴
and
single. ⁵

¹ *1000*: A strong group of people

² *10,000*: A very strong, powerful group. The stronger the group, the more the members exert pressure on a person to conform to their doctrine.

³ *They will stand on their feet*: They will be firm and strong against group pressure

⁴ *One:* Double meaning: 1) One with themselves and all; 2) united as brothers and sisters

⁵ *Single*: One with who they really are.

The Gospel Of Thomas

Poem 1
(22)

←↑→

Poem 3
(24)

Jesus
peered upon some
littleones
taking milk

And
he
said to his disciples:

"These little-ones[1]
taking milk[2]

They
are comparable
to those

Who
go inward
to the kingdom."

The disciples
responded:

Then
we
being
little-ones

We
will go inward
to the kingdom?"

Jesus
responded:

"When
you
should make the two

The one;[3]

[1] *Little-ones*: Those who are one and single with their core life

[2] *Taking milk*: Discovering wisdom on their own.

[3] *When you should make the two the one*: When you should leave your false selves and become one with your real self…

Jesus' disciples
said:

"Show us
to the place[1]

Where
you
are
there[2]

Because
it
is
necessary to us

That
we
seek after it."

Jesus
responded:

He

Who
has
his ear

Let him
listen.

"The light
exists inward
of a man
of light[3]

And
he
comes to be
light
to the world[4]

[1] *Place*: The center from which one thinks and acts.

[2] *Where you are there*: From where you live life

[3] *The light exists inward of a man of light*. The light exists inward to a man who has chosen to be his light.

[4] *He comes to be light to the world*: He comes to be light to the degree that he makes the two the one (see parallel Poem 1).

Chapter 7

And if
you
should make the
side
inward

Like
the side
outward

And
the side outward

Like
the side inward

And
the side
upper

Like
the side
lower[4]

And
not
the male
comes to be
a male

And so
you
will be making your
maleness
and
your femaleness
one
and
single[5]

All of it.

If
he
does
not come to be
light

The darkness
is
he."

[4] *"You you should make the side…."* When you do not identify with any side of an argument… You may hold a position in a debate, but not to the extent that you get upset with anyone.

[5] *And so you will be making your maleness and your femaleness one and single:* You do not identify with anything or anyone, not even with your gender.

The Gospel Of Thomas

Such that
not
the female
comes to be
a female;

And when
you
should make an eye

In place
of some eyes ⁶

And
a hand

In place
of a hand ⁷

And
a foot

In place
of a foot ⁸

And
an appearance

In place
of an appearance; ⁹

Then
you
will go inward
to the kingdom." ¹⁰

[6] *And when you should make an eye in place of some eyes*: And when you know all with a single soul-eye instead of using one eye to look at yourself and the other to peer out to see if you are meeting expectations.

[7] *And when you should make ... a hand in place of a hand*: A "hand" signifies "control." And when you do not identify with being in control or out of control of the situation...

[8] *And when you should make... a foot in place of a foot*: A "foot" signifies "the principles and beliefs that we stand on." And when you do not identify with your principles and beliefs...

[9] *And when you should make ... an appearance in place of an appearance*: And when you do not identify with how others perceive and judge you...

[10] *Then you will go inward to the kingdom*: Then, being free of false selves and all the anger, frustration, depression, anxiety and worry that you have caused by defending and promoting them, you will become the joyful, wise ruler of yourself and your interactions with others.

CHAPTER 15
SAYINGS: 66-68

Poem 2
(67)

He

Who
knows the all [1]

If
he
needs himself [2]

Then
he
needs the place [3]

All of it. [4]

[1] *All*: All contains the life of the Father and Mother, even those who live as dead people

[2] *If he needs himself*: If he needs his false self

[3] *Place*: Center of false consciousness in a person

[4] *All of it*: He needs all of it because he has nothing and he is being torn apart unconsciously. He knows the "all," and does not choose to be one with the "all."

Poem 1
(66)

← ↑ →

Show me
to the stone ¹

The one

That
they ²
turned away

Namely
by those

Who
build; ²

He
is
the corner stone. ³

¹ *Stone*: A person who speaks wise words.

² *They*: Dead people

² *Those who build*: Those leaders who build organizations that indoctrinate.

³ *He is the corner stone*: He is the person who will be the foundation of the kingdom in the world.

Poem 3
(68)

You
are
the blest ones ¹

When
they
hate you ²

And
persecute you ³

For
they
will discover
not any place ⁴

Where
you
have
not persecuted
yourselves. ⁵

¹ *Blest ones*: Those being given much by the Father and Mother

² *Hate you*: Hate the manifestation of life in you

³ *Persecute you*: Do things to destroy what they fear, what they are jealous of

⁴ *Place*: A death center within a person that has not been confronted and removed.

⁵ *For they will discover not any place where you have not persecuted yourselves*: They will not find a weakness in your character that you have not examined and eliminated.

Chapter 8
Sayings 25-33

Poem 5
(31)

No prophet [1]
is accepted
in his own village; [2]

No physician [3]
heals those

Who
know him. [4]

[1] *Prophet*: A person who soul-listens to the voice of God and speaks what he hears.

[2] *Village*: Group of dead people.

[3] *Physician*: An alive person

[4] *Those who know him*: Those dead people who know him superficially.

Poem 4
(29)

If
the flesh [1]

It
comes to be
because of spirit

A wonder
it
is. [2]

If
spirit
however

Comes to be
because of the body

A wonder
wondrous
it
is. [3]

Rather
I
myself
have come to be amazed
at this:

How
this great richness [4]

It
was placed
in this poverty. [5] [6]

[1] *Flesh*: A physical body.

[2] *Comes to be because of spirit, a wonder it is*: All is alive with divine life, how wonderful.

[3] *If spirit…a wonder wonderous it is*. The body enables the spirit to be born—how wonderful.

[4] *Richness*: Life

[5] *Poverty*: Lack

[6] *Come to be amazed… in this poverty*: I have come to be amazed that infinite life and wisdom could be placed in me, who has hardly begun to live it fully.

Poem 6
(30)

The place [1]

Which
has
three gods
there

In God
they
are.

The place

Which
has
two or one
there

I
myself
exist with him. [2]

[1] *Place*: The life center from which one thinks and acts.

[2] *(I do not understand this poem)*

Chapter 8

Poem 3
(27)

If
you
do
not fast
from the <u>world</u>[1]

You
will discover
not
the kingdom.[2]

If
you
do
not make the
Sabbath
outward[3]
the Sabbath
inward[4]

You
will <u>peer</u>[5]
<u>not</u>
upon the <u>Father</u>.[6]

[1]*World*: All of the people who embrace living divided between their real and false selves.

[2]*If you…you will discover not the kingdom*: If you try to live with divided people, and at the same time, live without division within yourself and between yourself and them, you will not succeed.

[3]*Sabbath outward*: A time devoted to stillness.

[4]*Sabbath inward*: A time of internal stillness. A time of living in the present rather than the past or future.

[5]*Peer*: Soul-see.

[6]*You will peer not upon the Father*: Unless you become soul-still, you will not third-eye see the real life and light in all.

← ↑ →

Poem 7
(28)

I
stood on my feet[1]
in the midst
of the <u>world</u>[2]

And
I
appeared to them
in flesh[3]

And
I
discovered them

All of them

Drunk;[4]

For
blind men[5]

They
are in their heart

And
they
<u>peer inward</u>[6]
<u>and outward</u>
<u>not</u>;

For
they
have come into the
world
empty[7]

And
they
also seek
to go out of the
world
empty.[8]

[1]*Stood on my feet*: Presented myself fully and strongly.

[2]*In the midst of the world*: In the midst of people lacking a high level of wisdom and life.

[3]*I appeared to them in flesh*: I tangibly demonstrated to them a high level of life and wisdom.

[4]*Drunk*: In a false awareness of themselves and the world.

[5]*Blind men*: Men who cannot third-eye peer upon the life of the Father and Mother.

[6]*Peer*: To soul-observe the true nature of someone or something.

[7]*Empty*: Lacking false selves as a little child. Lacking an ego.

[8]*They also seek to go out of the world empty*: We come into the world empty of ego, and we go out empty because we have created a great ego.

But
now
they
are
drunk. ⁹

⁹ *Drunk*: Dead unconscous

When
they
should throw-off
their wine¹⁰

¹⁰ *Wine*: Life. Here, false life.

Then
they
will repent.¹¹

¹¹ *Repent*: Admit that they have chosen a false life.

Chapter 8

Poem 2
(25)

←↑→

Poem 8
(26)

Love your <u>brother</u> ¹ ²

Like
your soul; ³

Guard him ⁴

Like
the pupil ⁵
of your <u>eye</u>. ⁶

¹ *Brother*: One who possess divine life. Every person, animal, plant and thing—all possess at their core the life of the Mother and Father.

² *Love your brother*: Be a twin of all.

³ *Soul*: We are all unique manifestations of one life.

⁴ *Guard him*: Protect and attack threats to your brothers.

⁵ *Pupil*: Core.

⁶ *Like the pupil of your eye*: Like the life center of your being which soul-sees.

The spec ¹

Which
is in the <u>eye</u>
of your <u>brother</u> ²

You see it.

The beam

Which
is in your <u>eye</u>

You
see
not
it.

When
you
should throw the beam
outward of your <u>eye</u>

Then
you
will see
outward
to throw the spec
outward
of the <u>eye</u>
of your <u>brother</u>.

¹ *Spec*: The small sign of death

² *Brother*: Everyone.

The Gospel Of Thomas

Poem 1
(32)

← ↑ →

Poem 9
(33)

A city[1]
is being built
upon a mountain[2]

It
raised up[3]

It
fortified[4]

In no way
That
it
might fall[5]

Nor
can
it
be hidden.[6]

[1]*City*: An individual or a group of people full of life and wisdom.

[2]*Mountain*: A person who is a twin of the core life in all. He has made the "two" the "one."

[3]*Raised up*: It fully visible.

[4]*Fortified*: Guarded from the influence of dead people.

[5]*Fall*: Be overthrown by dead people

[6]*Nor can it be Hidden*: The dead will not see the life in those in the kingdom; however, they will view their disruption of the world.

He[1]

Who
you
will listen to
with your inward
and your outward ear

Preach him
upon your housetops.[2]

For
does
not
anyone
burn a lamp[3][4]

And
he
put it
under an ear[5]

Nor
does
not
he
put it
in a place
hidden.

Rather
he
puts it
upon a lampstand

So that
anyone

Who
goes inward
and goes outward[6]

May peer
upon its light.[7][8]

[1]*He*: He alive and wise.

[2]*Housetops*: A house is each of us.

[3]*Burn*: To make painful. Words from Spirit "burn," that is, cause pain to those who resist them.

[4]*Lamp*: Source of real light.

[5]*Under an ear*: Where one cannot soul-listen to him.

[6]*Goes inward and goes outward*: In another poem, Jesus says that the "kingdom is of the eye inward and of the eye outward." So, one who goes inward and outward is soul-knowing himself, others and the world.

[7]*May peer upon its light*: So that those seeking the kingdom can learn from one in the kingdom.

[8]*Poem meaning*: Jesus states a law of being: Those alive will be a guide to others, and they will disrupt the world.

CHAPTER 14
SAYINGS: 64-65

Poem 2
(65a)

A just man[1]
had
a place
of grapes[2]

And
he
gave it
to some tenants[3]

So that
they
might work on it[4]

And
he
take his fruit[5]
from their hand.[6]

He
sent
his servant[7]

So that
the tenants
might give to him
the fruit[8]
of the place
of grapes.

[1] *Just man:* The Father.

[2] *Place of grapes:* A place teaching people to be alive.

[3] *Tenants:* Leaders teaching the Way of Life.

[4] *Work on it:* Reect and discover the meaning of hidden wisdom that is needed for life.

[5] *Fruit:* The results of a full life: singleness, oneness with others, the ability to love/guard, etc.

[6] *Hand:* Ability to control

[7] *Servant:* A person who shares the life of the kingdom.

[8] *Fruit:* Characteristics of one living life. E.g. singleness, light, openness, oneness with others, and wisdom.

The Gospel Of Thomas

They
grabbed his servant

And
beat him[9]

[9]*Beat him:* Made him suffer for living life.

And
with a little more time

They
would have killed him.[10]

[10]*Would have killed him:* would have influenced him to give up his Way of Wisdom and Death and become a living dead man.

The servant
went

And
he
spoke
to his lord.

His lord
said:

"Perhaps
they
did
not know him."[11]

[11]*Did not know him:* Did not soulsee wisdom and life in him.

And so
he
sent another servant.

And
the tenants
beat him.

And so
the lord
sent his son[12]

[12]*Son:* A person living a very high level of life and wisdom. One united with the Father and Mother.

Chapter 14

And
he
said:

"Perhaps
they
will be ashamed
before him."

The tenants

Because
they knew

That
he
is
the heir
to the place
of grapes

Seized him

And
killed him.[13]

[13] *Killed him:* Taught him to be a dead man. (Perhaps Jesus was predicting his own death).

Poem 1
(64)

⟵↑⟶

Poem 3
(65a)

A man[1]
was having
visitors[2]

[1] *Man:* An alive person

[2] *Was having visitors:* Was wanting people who claimed to want life to share his wisdom and life.

And
when
he
had prepared the dinner[3]

[3] *Dinner:* Time to share food (wisdom)

He
sent his servant[4]

[4] *Servant:* Person who lives with him and who shares his wisdom and life.

So that
he
might <u>call</u> the visitors.[5]

[5] *Call his visitors:* Choose people.

He
went to the first

And
he
said to him:

"My Lord
<u>calls</u> you."

He
said:

"I
have money
for traders[6]

[6] *I have money for traders:* I have what dead people want in exchange for their allegiance to me.

They
are
coming to me
in the evening[7]

[7] *Evening:* Beginning of inner darkness.

And
I
will go there[8]

[8] *There:* To my inner place of darkness.

He
Who
has
his ear[1]

[1] *Ear:* Third ear for listening to a meal of wisdom.

Let him
also
<u>listen</u>.[2]

[2] *Listen:* Respond to the call to soul-know wisdom.

And
I
will place orders
with them ⁹

Therefore
I
beg off
going
to dinner." ¹⁰

He
went to another one

And
he
said to him:

"My lord
<u>calls</u> you."

He
said to him:

"I
have bought a house ¹¹

And
it
requires of me
a day's time ¹²

And
I
will be resting
not." ¹³

He
went
to another one

⁹ *I will place orders with them.* I will tell them what I want in exchange for their life of death.

¹⁰ *I beg off going to dinner.* I have found reasons for not soul-knowing wisdom from my Father and Mother.

¹¹ *I have bought a house.* I have paid the price for being filled with false selves.

¹² *It requires of me a days time.* To nourish my false selves, I need to devote time that I could be using to be open and clear to soul-know wisdom.

¹³ *I will be resting not:* I will be too busy to be still and in the beginning.

And
he
said to him:

"My lord
calls you."

He
said to him:

"My friend
will be married [14]

    And
    because
    it
    is
    I

Who
will make the dinner [15]

I
can come
not [16]

Therefore
I
beg off
going
to the dinner."

He
went to another one

And
he
said to him:

"My lord
calls you."

[14] *My friend will be married*: A person I value will become one with death.

[15] *Who will make the dinner*: Who will feed people with what they need to be confirmed in their darkness.

[16] *I can come not*: I choose not to be in communion with one alive.

He
said to him:

"I
have bought a farm [17]

And
I
am going
to take the taxes [18]

Therefore
I
can come
not."

The servant
went

And
he
spoke to his lord:

"Those

Who
you
have called
to the dinner

Have begged off."

The lord
said to his servant:

"Go outward
to the ways [19]

Those

Who
you
will discover on them [20]

[17] *I have bought a farm:* I have what is necessary to grow in death.

[18] *I am going to take taxes:* I am going to get my rewards for living death.

[19] *To the ways*: To the Ways of both life and death

[20] *Those who you will discover on them*: Invite anyone who wants life.

Bring them

So that
they
may dine.

The buyers
and
the traders [21]
may go
not inward
to the place
of my Father. [22]

[21] *The buyers and the traders:* The indoctrinators who are getting paid with death to teach people about life.

[22] *Place of my Father:* The inner place in which a person is one with "He who lives."

Chapter 9
Sayings 34-38

Poem 3
(35)

In no way
can
one
go into the house
of the strong [1]

And
take him
by force [2]

Unless
he
binds his hands; [3]

Then
he
will move him
out of his house. [4]

[1] *House of the strong*: A person who is alive and wise.

[2] *Take him by force*: Take his core life by pressuring him to conform to the thinking of the world.

[3] *Unless he binds his hands*: Unless he takes away a person's ability to control his own life.

[4] *Out of his house*: Out of his rule over himself.

Poem 2
(36)

Do
not be concerned
from morning
up
to evening [1]

And
from there

From evening
up
to morning

For what
it
is

That
you
will put upon your-
selves. [2]

[1] *From morning up to evening*: From a time when you are about to be alive to a time when you are about to die.

[2] *For what it is...put upon yourselves*: For what false identities you might adopt. For the money, people, doctrine and things that you will identify with to make you special.

← ↑ →

Poem 4
(37)

Jesus' disciples asked him:

"On which day [1]
will
you
appear to us? [2]

And
on which day
will
we
peer upon you?" [3]

Jesus responded:

"When
you
should strip yourselves
naked [4]
without being ashamed [5]

And
you
take your garments [6]

And
you
put them
on the earth [7]
under your feet [8]

Like
those little
small children [9]

And
you
trample them; [10]

Then
you
will peer upon the son
of He

[1] *Day*: Time of openness and clarity.

[2] *Will you appear to us*: Will you prove that you are special.

[3] *Will we peer upon you*: Will we see your core, light self with soul-knowing.

[4] *When you strip yourselves naked*: When you remove your false identities; when you stop thinking that money, people, doctrine and things make you special.

[5] *Without being ashamed*: Without worrying about whether you conform to the expectations of others.

[6] *Garments*: False selves.

[7] *Earth*: Our reflective consciousness. To put garments on the earth is to bring into consciousness one's false identifications and the harm they cause to oneself and others.

[8] *Feet*: What we stand on for confidence.

[9] *Little, small children*: People who are themselves, who have no false identities.

[10] *Trample them*: See those clothes (false identities) as foolish and useless. To trample is to demean what gave one false life.

Chapter 9

Who lives ¹¹

And
you
will come to be
<u>afraid
not</u>. ¹²

¹¹ You will peer upon the *son of He Who Lives*: You will reveal yourself and the core of another as the son or daughter of He Who Lives.

¹² *Come to be afraid not*: Come to not be afraid of people attacking one's false identities.

Poem 1
(34)

← ↑ →

Poem 5
(35)

<u>A blind man</u> ¹

<u>If
he
should convey
before him
a blind man</u> ²

They
will fall ³

The two
of them

They
down
into a pit. ⁴

¹ *Blind man*: A person who does not soul-know.

² *A blind man*: An indoctrinating leader

³ *They will fall*: They will become more blind.

⁴ *They down into a pit*: They will develop deeper and deeper death habits.

Many times
did
you
come to be
desirous
to listen
to these words

These
which
I
speak to you

And
<u>you
did
not have another</u> ¹
<u>from whom
to listen
from his hand</u>. ²

Some days ³
will come to be

And
you
will seek after me

And
you
will discover
not
me. ⁴

¹ *Did not have another*: Did not have one who was soul-seeing. You only had blind indoctrinating leaders.

² *To listen from his hand*: To listen to his carefully contrived speeches.

³ *Some days*: Some periods of openness and clarity.

⁴ *And you will discover not me*: You will not see me because you have developed habits of seeking from blind indoctrinators.

CHAPTER 13
SAYINGS:61-63

Poem 3
(62b)

That

Which
your right
will do

Let
not
your left
realize what

That
is. [1]

[1] *Poem Meaning:* Become so congruently one with your yourself that you have no concern for anything else.

Poem 2
(61)

→↑←

Poem 4
(63a)

*Jesus
said to Salome:*

"There
are
two

Who
will rest
there
on a dining-bed" [1] [2]

The one
will
die

And
the other
will live." [3]

*Salome
said:*

"You
are
who

You
man?

From where [4]
do
you
climb onto my
dining-bed

And
you
eat off of my table?"

*Jesus
said to her:*

[1] *Dining-bed*: At the time of Jesus, few houses had chairs. One lay on the floor or on a pad to eat.

[2] *Who will rest on a dining-bed*: Who will take time to share in a meal of wisdom with soul-knowing.

[3] *One will die, and the other will live*: One person will soul-listen and live, and the other will not soul-listen and die.

[4] *From where*: From what place within do you choose to dine, from the place of life or the place of death?

There
was
a man
of wealth [1]

Who
had
he
there [2]

He
many riches. [3]

*Said
he
this:*

"I
will make use
of my riches
by sowing
and reaping
and planting [4]

And
filling my treasure-
house [5]
with fruit [6]

So that
I
will
not need anything." [7]

*These
were his thoughts

That
were
there

They
in his heart.*

[1] *Man of wealth*: ¹⁾ A man who is one with his core life from the Father and Mother.

[2] *There*: In his inner place o flife

[3] *Many riches*: Much wisdom.

[4] *By...planting*: By doing what is necessary to get not more wisdom, but those things to be save, secure and confortable in death.

[5] *And filling my treasure-house*: And filling the core of my being.

[6] *With fruit*: With the rewards of living death.

[7] *So that I will not need anything*: So that in the future I will not worry.

Chapter 13

I
am
he

Who
exists outward
of He

Who
is
undivided.⁵

I
am given outward
of that ⁶
of my Father.

*Salome
said:*

"I
am
your disciple."

*Jesus
said:*

*Because
of your response*

I
speak to you
this:

"When
he ⁷
should come to be
destroyed ⁸

He
will be
full
of light.⁹

And
in the night ⁸

Which
was
there ⁹

He
died. ¹⁰

⁵ *Who exists out of He who is undivided.* Who exists out of He who lives. Who is one with the Father and Mother who are one with their real selves and one with the core life in all.

⁶ *Of that of my Father:* Of that life and wisdom of my Father.

⁷ *He*: A person seeking more life

⁸ *When he should come to be destroyed*: When he should destroy his false selves.

⁹ *Light:* That which which illuminates the darkness in all.

⁸ *In the night*: In that death confusion.

⁹ *Which was there*: Which he created as soon as he decided to make living for future safety in people and things his priority rather than living unconditional love-guarded in the moment.

¹⁰ *He died*: He became divided between his real self and his false self.

When
however
he
should come to be
divided [10]

He
will be
full
of darkness. [11]

[10] *When he should come to be divided:* When one should come to be divided between his real and false selves.

[11] *Darkness:* Death and confusion, opaque

Poem 1
(62a)

I
speak of my mysteries [1]
to those [2]

Who
are
worthy
of my mysteries.

[1] *My mysteries:* My wisdom about how to grow in life

[2] To those: To those who live from he who lives.

← ↑ →

Poem 5
(63b)

He [1]

Who
has
his ear

Let him
listen.

[1] *He:* He who lives from he who lives.

CHAPTER 10
SAYINGS 39-43

Poem 3
(42)

You
come to be[1]

As
you
pass away.[2]

[1]*Come to be:* Come to be fully alive

[2]*As you pass away:* As the death causing habits in you become less and less. We "pass away" as we lose our false identities.

←↑→

Poem 2
(40)

A vine
of grapes[1]
was planted
not
in the Father[2]

And
it
was fortified
not;[3]

It
will be pulled
up
by its root[4]

And
it
will be destroyed.[5]

[1]*A vine of grapes:* A person who has the potential to be more alive
[2]*Was planted not in the Father:* The person was taught (planted) to conform to the expectations of indoctrinators.
[3]*Fortified not:* The person was not shown how to protect himself from indoctrinating leaders.

[4]*It will be pulled up by its root:* He will be taken from his center in himself.

[5]*It will be destroyed:* He will suffer living death.

Poem 4
(41)

He
Who
has
it
in his hand[1]

It
will be given
to him.[2]

And
he
Who
has
not
it
in his hand[3]

The other
little bit

Which
has
he
in his hand

It
will be taken
from him.[4]

[1]*He who has it in his hand:* He who has the disciplined wisdom to grow daily in life.

[2]*It will be given to him:* More life and wisdom will be given to him.

[3]*He who has not in his hand:* He who wanders on the Way of Death.

[4]*It will be taken from him:* Gradually, he will die a thousand deaths. We do not drift. We either become more alive or more dead.

145

Poem 1
(39)

The Pharisees
and
the Scribes [1]
took the keys
of knowledge [2]

And
they
hid them [3]

Nor
did
they
go inward. [4]

And those

Who
desire
to go inward

They
did
not permit them. [5]

You
however
come to be
cunning
like serpents [6]

And
innocent
like doves. [7] [8]

[1] *Pharisees and Scribes:* Two of the many groups of clerics within Judaism. In this Gospel, they represent all indoctrinating leaders, whether religious or secular. Such leaders could be politicians, clerics, professors, parents, business managers, TV celebrities, or influential friends.

[2] *Keys of knowledge:* How to discover one's answers on one's own.

[3] *Hid them:* Taught people that they needed to get information from authorities.

[4] *Nor did they go inward:* Nor did they use soul-knowing to evolve in life.

[5] *They did not permit them:* The authorities taught people to distrust soul-knowing.

[6] *Cunning like serpents:* Wisely moving and working in the world without being part of it.

[7] *Innocent like doves:* Open, one with oneself, beautiful in spirit.

[8] *Cunning and innocent:* Two aspects of an evolved person. In Ch. 8, Pm. 2 Jesus speaks of those two aspects as "guarding" and "loving."

Poem 5
(43)

His disciples asked him:

"You
are
who

That
you
speak these things
to us?" [1]

Jesus responded:

"In those things

Which
I
speak to you

You
realize
not [2]

That
I
am
the who. [3]

You
have come to be
like
those Judeans [4]

For
they
love the tree [5]

And
they
hate its fruit [6]

[1] *You are who that you speak these things to us:* You play what authoritative role when you speak these wisdom sayings to us? Are you a "Pharisee, a "Scribe?"

[2] *You realize not:* You do not see my life because you are blinded by the beliefs of your indoctrinators.

[3] *I am the who:* I live from and with He who lives.
Throughout the Old Testament, people ask about the "who." Jesus speaks of himself and all alive in divine life as the answer to that question. E.g. Ps. 113: 5: "Who is like the Lord our God?" Or Isa. 28: 2 "Behold, the Lord has one who is mighty and strong."

[4] *Judeans:* Indoctrinating authorities, such as the Pharisees and Scribes.

[5] *Tree:* Tree of the knowledge life in the Garden of Eden.

[6] *Fruit:* The results of using the tree of the knowledge of life. Independence, congruence, love-guardedness, etc.

Chapter 10

And
they
love the fruit

And
they
hate the tree.⁷

[7] *Hate the tree*: Hate the internal change necessary to know with the tree of life.

CHAPTER 12
SAYINGS 51-60

Poem 5
(55)

Whoever
hates his father
not
and his mother [1]

He
will come to be
a disciple
not to me;

And
whoever
hates his brothers
and his sisters
not [2]

He
will come to be
not
worthy
of me.

[1] *Whoever hates his father not and his mother*: Whoever does not hate being the person he adopted when he identified with the beliefs, hopes, values and traditions of his parents.

[2] *Whoever hates his brothers and sisters not*: Whoever does not hate the false identities given to him by everyone.

←→

Poem 6
(56)

Whoever
has known the world [1]
has discovered a corpse. [2]

And
whoever
has discovered a corpse

The world
is
worthy
of him
not.

[1] *World*: People with false identities.

[2] *Corpse*: People dead

Poem 4
(54)

The blest
are
the poor [1]

For
yours
is
the kingdom
of the heavens. [2]

[1] *Poor*: Those without false identities

[2] *Kingdom of the heavens*: A "kingdom" is a way of being. Thus, one living in a "kingdom of heavens" understands all in a high way, closer to God's view of all. We can only do that when we rid ourselves of our false identities.

←→

Poem 7
(57)

The kingdom
of the Father [1]

It
is
like a man [2]

Who
had
he
there
a seed
good. [3]

[1] *Kingdom of the Father*: A person ruling over himself and his interactions with others as does the Father.

[2] *Man*: A person seeking to grow in life.

[3] *Who had he there a seed, good*: Who had he there a wise insight.

149

The Gospel Of Thomas

His enemy
came in the night[4]

And
he
sowed a weed[5]
upon the seed
good.

The man
did
not permit them[6]
to pull up the weed;[7]

And
he
said to them:

"Do
not pull up the weed

For
you
will pull up
the <u>grain</u>[8]
with it;

For
on the day
of the harvest[9]

The weeds
will appear outward

And
they
will be pulled up

And
they
will be burned."[10]

[4]*Night:* Time of difficulty and confusion.

[5]*Weed:* False solution or belief

[6]*Them:* Others or the parts of himself that wanted to rush things.

[7]*Pull up the weed*: To remove the false idea.

[8]*Grain:* The tangible results of living on the Way of Life.

[9]*Day of the harvest:* Time when the person sees clearly how to separate himself from his false identities.

[10]*The weeds will appear... and they will be burned:* The person will rid himself of false identities at the appropriate time in his own way.

Poem 3
(53)

↔

Poem 8
(58)

*His disciples
asked him
this:*

"Circumcision [1]

It
is
beneficial
or not to us?"

*He
said to them
this*:

"If
it
were beneficial

Their Father
would beget them
out of their mother
circumcised.

Rather
circumcision
true in spirit [2]
has found merit

All of it.

[1] *Circumcision*: Removing the old and useless.

[2] *Circumcision true in Spirit*: The removal of our troubles (false identities) is the true spirit.

A blest one
is
the man

Who
is
troubled [1]

For
he
has discovered life. [2]

[1] *Who is troubled*: Who is troubled by how he lives death.

[2] *Discovered life*: When we see the old, destructive pattern in our life, it is because we see it against a new more "heavenly" way to be. We can now remove those old ways, that is, we can circumcise ourselves (see Poem 3).

Poem 2
(52)

→←

Poem 9
(59)

*His disciples
said to him:*

"Twenty four prophets [1]
spoke in Israel

And
they
spoke

All of them

About <u>you</u>."

[1] *Prophets*: People who predicted the future Messiah King

Watch
for <u>he</u>

Who
<u>lives</u>

While
<u>you</u>
are living;

Lest
you
<u>die</u>

*He
said to them
this*:

"You
have given up
on he

Who
lives
in your presence ²

And
you
have spoken about those

Who
are
dead." ³

And
you
seek
to see him

And
you
can find the power
not. ¹

² *He who lives in your presence*: The disciples have such strong, false beliefs about the Messiah King that they cannot see him fully alive in front of them.

³ *You have spoken about those who are dead.* The prophets did not leave religious and secular doctrine fully, nor did they enable others to leave it. Instead, they remained divided. Like John the Baptist, they tried to maintain the old and the new at the same time (recall Poem Nine in this Chapter). Thus, they did not become "little-children" who are alive.

¹ *Can find the power not*: Only the living can soul-know those living. To the degree that one is dead, to that degree he will never recognize life in another, nor will he visualize a higher way to be.

Chapter 12

Poem 1
(51)

⟵⟶

Poem 10
(60)

His disciples asked him:

"On which day
is
the <u>stillness</u> [1]
for those

Who
are
<u>dead</u> [2]

It
coming to be.

And
on which day
is
the world new

It
coming to be?" [3]

He said to them this:

"The it
for which
you
watch outward

It
has come [4]

Rather
you
know
not it. [5]

[1] *Stillness*: repose. Last Judgment.

[2] *Dead*: Physically dead

[3] *World new, it coming to be*: The O.T. prophets said that at the "end of times," a Messiah King will come and establish a "new" world order.

[4] *It has come*: Your peace and new order exists whenever you want to choose it. I am an example.

[5] *You know not it*: And you and others choose not to see me and the light and life at your core.

They saw a Samaritan [1]

He taking a lamb [2] *to himself*

He going into Judea. [3]

Jesus said to his disciples this:

"That one

He
is
<u>close to the lamb</u>." [4]

They said to him this:

"He
does that

So that
he
might <u>kill</u> him

And
he
might eat him." [5]

Jesus said to them this:

[1] *Samaritan*: Many Jews saw the Samaritans as practicing a heretical form of Judaism.

[2] *Lamb*: A symbol of a person who is a little child full of life.

[3] *Judea*: Symbol of both a controlling religion and traditions.

[4] *He is close to the lamb*: He helps the lamb to remain still.

[5] *So that he might kill him and he might eat him*: He quiets the lamb so that he can more easily kill him and eat him. False leaders give quieting messages to their constituents so that they might lead them into death doctrine.

"While
he
lives

He
will eat him
not⁶

Rather
if
he
should kill him

And
he
comes to be
a corpse."⁷

They
said:

"In another way

He
can do it
not."⁸

He
said to them
this:

"You
also
seek a place
for yourselves
in stillness⁹

So that
you
not
come to be
corpses

And
they
eat you."¹⁰

⁶*While he lives, he will not eat him*: While a person lives life, an indoctrinator (cleric, peer pressure, politician, media person, etc.) cannot steal his soul.

⁷*Rather if he should kill him and he comes to be a corpse.* Rather, if the indoctrinator should render him unconscious in doctrine, removing his beautiful, independent life.

⁸*In another way he can do it not*: An indoctrinator needs to brain wash (kill) a person, or he cannot seduce him and render him into a robot.

⁹*You also seek a place for yourselves in stillness*: You also seek to be alive and all powerful in the moment.

¹⁰*And they eat you*: And they destroy you by leading you into doctrinaire darkness.

CHAPTER 11
SAYINGS 44-50

Poem 4
(48)

Should
two
make peace
with each other
in this house
unified [1]

They
will speak
to the mountain [2]
this:

"Move"

And
it
will move.[3]

[1] *Should two make peace with each other in this house unified:* Should a person make peace with his false self and become unified.

[2] *Mountain:* A highly still, powerful person who identifies with the core life in himself and others; thus, he is the "twin" of himself and others.

[3] *Move and it will move:* In his stillness, a mountain person commands himself to move in the world.

Poem 3
(46)

Part 1

From Adam
up to John
the Baptist [1]
among the
begotten
of women

No one
has been raised up
above John the
Baptist

[1] John the Baptist: A close friend and cousin of Jesus.

←Part 1
←→

Poem 5
(47)

In no way

Can
a man
climb onto horses
two [1]

And
he
stretch bows two.[2]

[1] *Horses two:* A horse represents power. Within us are two powers. One from Light and the other from the dark selves we create.

[2] *Stretch bows two:* A bow is strong intention. Within us is the intention to live more life or to live more death.

So that
he
need lower his
eyes. ²

Part 2

I
speak
however
this:

"He

Who
will come to be
among you

He
being
a little-one

He
will know the
kingdom

And
he
will be raised up
above John."³

² *No one has been raised up above John*: John was righteous above all according to the Torah Laws.

³ *He who will come to be...will be raised up above John*: He who will leave his false identifications with religious laws, such as the Torah, will be alive like a little one. John did not do that; thus, he was great as measured by the Torah, but not as measured by the life in one free of false identifications.

←Part 2
→←

In no way
can
a servant
serve lords two ³

Or
he
will honor the one

And the other one
he
will despise.

No man
drinks wine
old

And immediately
he
desires
to drink wine
new. ⁴

And
they
do
not pour wine
new
into wineskins
old

So that
they
not split open.⁵

³ *Lords two*: We can follow two kinds of leaders: The first is He who lives within us. The second are those to whom we honor by living up to their expectations.

⁴ *No man drinks wine old and desires to drink wine new*: A person does not take in old, dead beliefs, and immediately desire to take in new life wisdom.

⁵ *They do not pour wine new into wineskins old so that they not split open*: One does not combine death living with live living without splitting himself in two with confusion and anxiety, and ...

Chapter 11

And
they
do
not pour <u>wine</u>
<u>old</u>
into <u>wineskins</u>
<u>new</u>

So that
it
not be destroyed. ⁶

And
they
do
not sow <u>patches</u>
<u>old</u>
on <u>garments</u>
<u>new</u>

Because
there
a split
will come to be. ⁷

⁶ *Do not pour wine old into wine new...so that it not be destroyed:* If you try to put the logic of living life and wisdom into a person living death and ignorance, you will be left with death and destruction.

⁷ *Do not sow patches old on garments new, because there a split will come to be:* A garment is a self projected into the world. Those dead project a false self. Those alive, a real self. One may try to project realness and parts of the old, false self; however, doing so will split one emotionally.

Poem 2
(45)

Grapes [1]
are
not harvested
out of thorns [2]

Nor
do
they
gather figs [3]
out of thistles [4]

For
they
do
not yield fruit. [5]

A good man
brings good things [6]
out of his treasure

And
an evil man
brings evil things
out of his treasure [7]

Which
is
wicked

Which
is
in his heart

And
from which
he
speaks evil things.

For
out of the excess
of the heart
does
he
bring out
evil things.

[1] *Grapes*: Real life

[2] *Thorns*: Attachments to people, doctrine and things.

[3] *Figs*: Sweet, nourishing life.

[4] *Thistles*: Dogma.

[5] *Fruit*: Life benefits

[6] *Brings good things out of his treasure*: Brings congruence, oneness, love-guardedness out of his store of wisdom.

[7] *An evil man brings evil things out of his treasure*: A dead man brings confusion and duplicity out of his treasure.

Poem 6
(49)

Those blest ones

They
are
the single ones [1]
and
the chosen ones [2]

For
you
will discover the
kingdom

For
you
are out
of it [3]

And again
you
will be going
there. [4]

[1] *Single ones*: Congruent ones.

[2] *Chosen ones*: Our Mother chooses to give life.

[3] *For you are out of it.* We were not born in sin, but as kings and queens living the life of our Mother and Father.

[4] *You are out of it, and you will be going there.* You were born alive, you died because you were indoctrinated into living false selves. To the degree that you choose to rid yourself of those false selves, to that degree you return to the life you had when you were born.

Chapter 11

Poem 1
(44)

⟷

Poem 7
(50)

Anyone

Who
blasphemes the
Father

Will be forgiven.

Anyone

Who
blasphemes the
son [1]

Will be forgiven. [2]

Whoever
blasphemes the
Spirit [3]

Which
is
holy [4]

Will
not be forgiven

Neither
on earth [5]

Nor
in heaven. [6]

[1] *Son*: One living the Life and Light of the Father and Mother.

[2] *Forgiven*: Freed to be what one really is.

[3] *Spirit*: One's spirit is the source of real clarity, wisdom and life.

[4] *Holy*: Blessed.

[5] *On earth*: In one's reflective consciousness.

[6] *Heaven*: In one's ability to realize a high level of knowing.

If
they
*should ask you
this:*

"You
have
come into being
from where?" [1]

*Speak to them
this:*

"We
have come
outward
of the Light [2]

The place [3]

Where
the Light
comes to be
there
outward
by its own hand. [4]

It
stood itself
on its own feet

And
it
appeared outward
in *its* appearances."
[5]

*If
they
should ask you
this:*

"Are
you
it?"

[1] *From where?* From which of the two spirits, the Holy Spirit or the spirit of the world?.

[2] *Light*: The blessed Spirit, the Spirit of real life and wisdom.

[3] *Place*: Center from which one thinks and acts.

[4] *By its own hand*: Under its own control.

[5] *In its appearances*: In its tangible manifestations.

Say this:

"We
are
<u>its</u> sons

And
we
are
the chosen
of the Father

Who
lives."

*If
they
should ask you
this:*

"What
is
the sign
of your Father

Which
is
in you?"

Say to them
this:

"<u>It</u>
is
movement

And
<u>it</u>
is
stillness. [5]

[5] *It is movement, and it is stillness*: The tangible characteristics of one who lives from the Light.

APPENDIX ONE

A Way of the Soul Primer

INTRODUCTION

The Way of the Soul begins with a person who seeks to leave the "world" in order to live more in the "kingdom."

The "world" is the life that most people live. It consists of

- Living mentally in the past and future.
- Living from sadness to happiness, from worry to relief, from depression to elation, from failure to success…on and on.
- Living the beliefs of others, and not being congruent with one's inner voice.

Summary: The "world" is "religion," not just theological religion, but of the way we make external beliefs more important than listening to one's intuitive voice or Voice.

Jesus uses the image and concept of "kingdom" as a *fulfilled way of being*, that is, a Way to experience oneself and life very differently than those in the "world."

To be concrete: In the kingdom, one lives in a type of bliss world that few understand. We are familiar with similar, short-term worlds. For example, falling in love is like entering a new world. It provides feelings of exhilaration and completeness and oneness—much like what it feels to be living in the kingdom. But this (falling in love) is a short-term world unless the new lovers find a way to continue living in that zone, that space, that way of being *every minute for the rest of their lives*. For most of us, that does not happen. Why? Because unless we live on the Way of the Soul, we cannot do it. We cannot maintain that level of relationship because our comfortable behaviors, thoughts, needs and even objects draw us away from the soul living, the joy, the exhilaration we experienced while falling in love. We want to stay in that space, but we can't. We feel a deep pull from within that draws us to that zone, makes us aware that we want it, but we cannot seem to maintain that feeling. That is why we see people trying to artificially create a "kingdom" by substituting activities for "falling in love," such as engaging in extra-marital affairs, watching pornography, dreaming while listening to romantic music, trying novel sex encounters, and using drugs that provide a "high."

According to Jesus, we all experience some aspects of the kingdom when we are tiny children—before we before we learn about roles and rules and titles. As we grow and are indoctrinated into our culture by family, teachers, and other leaders, we move further from the kingdom.

It's not a conscious occurrence. It's just how we are taught to live by those around us who are not on the Way of the Soul. But deep inside, we remember the experience of the kingdom as a child and long to live it again.

As one gradually lives more "in the kingdom," he will become a wise king (or queen) over his "field," which includes all aspects of himself as well as all of his interactions with others. Further, a "kingdom" for Jesus is also a group of people who live the Way of the Soul. He intended to invite everyone in the universe to be on that common Way to peace and fulfillment.

Seeking the "kingdom" is a goal for which a person must be willing to sacrifice anything and everything—especially his ego. He must "leave all" of his present dogma to follow the Way of the Soul, or he will choose a thousand psychological deaths. One cannot live with "one foot in and one foot out." To do so would cause great internal conflict and emotional and spiritual pain that would also radiate out to and affect all those within that individual's "field."

Through his Gospel, Jesus teaches the disciplined steps to achieving our deepest wish—to be back in the kingdom 24/7. This chapter provides a concise "primer" to living the Way of the Soul.

First, in order to *refresh* your experience of the "kingdom," permit me to lead you through an exercise.

Exercise

Look back over your life and recall your strongest "all experience." It was a moment or short span of time in which you were in the "now" and were one with all. Time seemed to stop. You enjoyed just being you and being with all around you—perhaps with your friend, your child, or the sunset. Some folks have that kind of experience on the last day of a vacation or a long weekend. Some folks have it when they take time to step away from everything and everyone and take a walk or sit on a swing or float in a body of water.

Maybe you can recall times when you acted from the "now" and enjoyed those wonderful emotions and thoughts of joy, personal power and safety. (Many have learned to act from the "now" in a practice commonly called "mindfulness." I think it should be called "soulfulness.")

However you have reached that experience, think about it now.

Now, in your imagination, put yourself back in that "all experience" and recall its details. Let me guide you:

Recall the stillness within you and around you. People may have been talking near you, but you were in a stillness bubble.

Recall that you felt emotionally healthy. You were not anxious, worried, depressed, sad, or in out-of-the-body excitement.

Appendix One

Recall how joy bubbled up from your soul.

Recall how alive you felt and how alive everything around you seemed. If you were sitting on the beach, for example, recall how the sea, the sand, the sky, and those around you seemed so real in a refreshing "alive" way.

Recall that you could sit or stand there and enjoy things that you normally never even saw. For example, if you were in a park, recall how you enjoyed feeling the breeze and watching it move the leaves of the trees. Remember how everything seemed to slow down (of course, it was actually you that slowed down!).

Recall how your ideas bubbled up from you soul. They seemed to come *through* you. You were not *manufacturing* them with your mind. You sensed the ideas or visions and then, secondarily, used your mind to shape and play with them.

Recall that your soul-ideas led you to plan something in the future. However, you planned from being in the present. You did not plan from a mind *anxious* about the future.

Recall that you were *in* the flow. Everything came effortlessly to you, and you decided easily to go this way or that. Perhaps in the park, you sensed to walk to the right. You did that and saw something wonderful that seemed to have been given to you, such as new kind of flower.

Sitting again, recall how you seemed to be one with universal intelligence (which you may have called, "my higher self," "my source," or "God.")

Recall that that intelligence *lovingly* guided your thoughts and your actions, such as to the new type of flower.

Recall the sense that you were infinitely loved.

Recall the sense that you were safe, no matter what happened.

Recall that as soon as a question arose from you soul, it was followed by the answer—tailored specifically for you.

Recall that you had suspended your mind and its beliefs. You were living from your experience, not from your faith in yourself, in God, or in any of the "truths" that you were taught. You had given up the Way of the Mind and entered the Way of the Soul.

If you were aware of God's presence, recall how you experienced and accepted it and without feeling a need to believe.

Recall that you enjoyed and appreciated your body. When you looked down at your hands, you were one with them. Your physical self and your spiritual self were singular, fluid and vibrating as one with the universe.

Recall saying to yourself, "I wish I could live like this forever—with no worries, fears or regrets."

Recall that you sensed yourself as a unique gift to the world.

Recall the realization that others were also unique gifts but that they did not seem to act like they were. Most were always trying to manufacture themselves.

Recall the peace, the quiet, the beauty, and the wonder of it "all."

Recall that deep down you sensed that nothing happens by accident, by luck, or by coincidence. Under those impressions of disorder, you sensed loving order.

Recall how the exact right events, things and people had "shown up" in your life almost magically, at the right time and place, and with exactly what you needed.

Recall how you sensed that the universe seemed to know what you most deeply needed before your mind did. How things, people and ideas came into your life without you even asking.

Recall how you remembered your hardships, such as people who betrayed you, your mistakes, and all of your problems. Recall how you saw that they all led you closer to what you most deeply wanted.

Recall how you realized that when you felt upset in the past, all of your feelings, ideas and actions emanated primarily from your mind, not your soul.

Recall how you noticed that when you were upset, all of your "mind" ideas led eventually to more upset.

Recall how you noticed that to get out of the vicious upset cycle, you needed to take time to be still in what Jesus calls "the beginning," that is, the "now."

Maybe you can recall times when that you acted from the "now" and were led to more of those wonderful emotions and thoughts of joy, personal power, and safety.

Recall how you may have said in your own way, "I create what will happen. From regret and worry, my mind guides me to more of the same suffering. From stillness and joy, my soul guides me to more wondrous fulfillment."

Reflections
You may not recall all of those specifics of the "All Experience." However, that is find if you remember a few. As one seeks the "All Experience" and studies it from inside, one usually disocveres many more aspects than those that I mentioned. As one does that, he seeks to live

the "All Experience" or "Kingdom" continually. Gradually under every thought and activity, he will be living from the kingdom and seeking to be more in it. That is the Way of the Soul.

The "Kingdom" or "All experience," then, is an *experience*, that is, "a way of being" in which one rules over himself and his interactions from his soul knowing, not his mental manipulations. It is also a community of people who are kings and queens. To enter that "space" or "zone," you suspended your faith in all that you believed in order to reenter your experience as a little child would. You leave your theological and social rules and dogmas to be your real you. You leave what Jesus called the "world," the "dead," the "body," and "darkness." You leave your emotional rollercoaster to be still and one with all. As a result, you began living "life" and "light."

Now, you know that Jesus did not set out to or actually start a religion. His desire, intention and actions were to free people from their mental religions so that they could be one with their real soul-selves and with all as the "kingdom." Now, you can go back through his ideas, sit with your soul, listen to others on the Way of the Soul, and discover your own, unique way of living the kingdom.

The Logic of the Two Ways

Jesus recognized why we are not in the kingdom 24/7: We are all blinded by our precious blind beliefs. He describes how we disempower ourselves with our blind beliefs in his "Parable of the Sower" (Chapter 2, Poem 1):

Behold![1]

He
went out

Namely
he

The one

Who
sows.[2]

And
he
filled his hand[3]
(with seed)[4]

[1] *Behold:* Soul-see! or third-eye see

[2] *The one who sows:* The one who provides seeds of wisdom (as Jesus does in these poems). Our soul v(V)oice.

[3] *Hand:* The ability to control.

[4] *Filled his hand:* From all of his ideas, he carefully chose his seeds of wisdom.

And
he
threw them.⁵

And
some
were
indeed
discovered
on the way.⁶

And
they
came

Namely
the birds⁷

And
they
gathered them.⁸

⁵*Threw them:* Confronted others with them.

⁶*Some were discovered on the way:* Some seeds of wisdom were heard by a person on the Way to higher levels of life.

⁷*They came, namely the birds:* The old blind-beliefs of the person came forward in the person's mind.

⁸*And they Gathered them:* The listener made his blind-beliefs more important than the wisdom.

In Jesus' parable of the sower, a wise man (symbolizing our soul v(V)oice) throws out seeds of wisdom on the "earth" (our reflective consciousness). "Birds" (blind beliefs) come and remove the seeds before they can grow. In other words, like fools, we choose to believe our dogma rather than suspend it to consider wisdom bubbling up from our soul. The Parable of the Sower is an example of how Jesus criticizes blind beliefs.

Religion rewards steadfast faith. Jesus preaches the opposite: doubt your beliefs and discover for yourself what is real. In that process, grow into being a wise child living 24/7 in the kingdom.

We are like people with layers of cataracts on their eyes. Each layer is a blind belief. We think we see reality when we actually see a composite distortion. We are in a false, "dead" "world." If we could see properly ourselves, others, and the true way that the universe works, we would be full of "life" in the kingdom 24/7. So, to get into the kingdom, we need to remove our cataracts, one blind belief at a time.

Appendix One

The problem: we identify with our beliefs and not our soul wisdom. Each of us is a unique version of a universal soul that is one with infinite intelligence (God). Each moment we have the option of living from that soul or from the blind beliefs in our mind. In other words, we choose every second to be on the Way of the Soul of the Way of the Mind. Because we identify with our beliefs, suspending and removing them threatens us. We feel vulnerable, and we are until we reveal a reality closer to the truth. Then we become a bit more a wise "king" or "queen" over ourselves and our interactions with others.

When a child is born, he sees more the kingdom than we do. He loves cartoons because they are closer to the reality that is the kingdom. He is fragile and unwise, but he lives the kingdom more than we do. Our job is to be a child again but with the power and wisdom to guard ourselves from adult indoctrination.

A child loses his kingdom vision and his connection with his soul as he embraces mental blind beliefs. Little by little, he grows faith cataracts. He learns to trust those mental filters more than his child, clear vision.

Theological, political, and other social religions exist when two or more people agree that a blind belief cataract is reality. People in that religion, then, think that they are special because they see absolute truth and others do not. They, then, may think that anyone who does not embrace their truths are wrong, bad, and even worthy of punishment. Religions, therefore, are the reason we do not live in the kingdom 24/7 and why we do not live as powerful, wise children, one with each other.

In the Gospel of Thomas and in his New Testament parables and core sayings (those that we find in two or more gospels), Jesus never uses the words "believe" or "faith" without being critical of that way of construing reality. He never preached a creed or a legal system, nor did he establish a hierarchy of authorities to enforce them. In no way did he establish a religion. His goal was to remove people from body/mind slavery, not to create another version of it.

In Thomas, instead of the word "believe," Jesus uses the words "discover" and "reveal." We remove our blind belief cataracts by "discovering" or "revealing" the nature of reality. Truths are embedded in reality, they are not in our secular and theological religious beliefs about reality. Therefore, the process of personal evolution out of blind belief "darkness" involves challenging and suspending our current beliefs so that our soul intuition can present us with what is real.

Jesus modeled an enlightened leader in his poems, parables and core sayings. Instead of teaching dogma, he taught people how to challenge doctrine and indoctrinators so that they can discover their own answers on their own. He describes our world-wide, religion-logic situation so powerfully and clearly in Chapter 10, Poem 1 (Saying 39):

The Gospel Of Thomas

Jesus
said this:

The Pharisees
and
the Scribes[1]
took the keys[2]
of knowledge,[3]

And
they
hid them,[4]

Nor
did
they
go inward;[5]

And those

Who
desired to go
inward,

They
did
not permit them.[6]

[1] *Pharisees and Scribes*: Two of the many groups of clerics within Judaism. In this Gospel, they represent all indoctrinating leaders, whether religious or secular. Such leaders could be politicians, clerics, professors, parents, business managers, TV celebrities and influential friends.

[2] *Keys*: The keys to knowledge are what Jesus teaches, beginning with soul-knowing.

[3] *Knowledge*: Knowledge of your real self, the real self of others, and the principles of coming alive in a dead world.

[4] *Hid them*: Taught people to make the beliefs of authorities more important than what they soul-know.

[5] *Go inward*: Leave their indoctrination and soul-know.

[6] *They did not permit them*: The authorities taught people to distrust soul-knowing.

Appendix One

The enslaving logic of religion permeates society, particularly our educational systems. We pay "Pharisees" (clerics, teachers, professors and lecturers) to proclaim truths, rather than to empower people to "discover" and "reveal" their own truths. We design churches, temples, lecture halls and classrooms so that the high priests can dominate from above the ignorant masses. We devise grading systems that divide students into good ones and bad ones. We abuse children by instilling in them fear of failure in the learning process. In those ways, we invite unconsciously the sick logic of religion into our minds. Is it any wonder that people live in free-floating regret, anxiety and worry?

Can people learn from experts? Certainly—after they have been empowered to challenge them. Would it not be wonderful if each of our clerics, politicians, teachers and talking heads stood up and proclaimed, "My primary job is to empower you to challenge every so-called truth that has ever been uttered, particularly by me."

Procedures for Becoming More "the Kingdom"

Every day, in every instant, we choose to ride one horse or the other, to serve one master or the other: the Way of the Soul or the Way of the Mind. Permit me to share some of the ways that people on the Way of the Soul live to be more in the kingdom.

Seek

A Soul person asks continually: Am I in the kingdom or not? When one is upset in any way (anxious, worried, feeling guilty or like a failure, or seeking excitement, food or shopping as an escape), he knows that he is not in the kingdom.

He, then, goes to a place where he can be still, usually a place apart from others (maybe a corner of a coffee shop or to a park). There he asks, "What have I chosen that makes me upset—please tell me". He is seeking answers from his soul voice (or Voice). He resists using his mind for solutions. He knows that his mental beliefs have caused him to be upset. He may remind himself that a little child seldom gets upset because he lives from his soul, not from artificial, indoctrinated faith in theology, money, friends, job, family, self-importance, etc.

When one begins communicating with his soul-voice (Source), he begins what seems impossible: communicating in a normal give and take conversation with God or with universal intelligence. Jesus modeled that, not to say that he was special, but to teach everyone to do it. He called his Voice his "Mother and Father." Each person can ask, "What do you want me to call you?" or any other questions, such as, "Who are you?" or "Are you a person?" or "Do you love me personally?" He then "listens" or "senses" words, images, and impressions bubbling up from his soul. When he hears things that he normally would not say to himself, he becomes surer that he is not imagining things.

Communicating with one's source or Source is a skill. Children do it naturally. We need to relearn the ability. Each person develops his own way and his own rules for determining whether he is creating both sides of the conversation or only his side. It is a highly rewarding skill to learn, because you find that you are never alone without someone who can give you answers—sometimes that you do not like—but answers to any question.

The core trick is to be empty of all agendas and detached from all former beliefs. Those agendas and, especially, common sense cultural beliefs, interfere with unbiased listening. Further, if one already thinks he knows the answer, he will not be open to being taught.

The Soul person may, then, begin reading Jesus' poems until one poem or line resonates with him or causes an "a-ha moment." Sometimes it seems like a word or line stands out from the others. That can be the soul's signal that that word or line is part of what you are immediately seeking. So, one way your soul voice breaks through the mental bedlam is by guiding you to an author who is on the Way of the Soul and who speaks something that resonates with you.

The Soul person may also listen to the lyrics of a song, or look at a billboard, or overhear a conversion (it could be *any* kind of input, really), because he knows that his soul will use anything or anyone to deliver the needed insight.

The Soul person may also seek help from a "soul" friend or therapist. If a friend or therapist is living from his mind, he probably will cause more confusion. One wants to find someone who helps the Soul person find his own answers. Only the soul knows the exact next step to take, be it an insight or an action.

The Soul person watches every thought or image that bubbles up from his soul. He turns it this way and that to uncover the needed insight.

If still upset, the Soul person may return to normal activities while continuing third-ear (soul) listening for his breakthrough idea.

Finding

A Soul Seeker listens for a few *general patterns* that cause upset. Let me list some.

- A Seeker checks to see if he is in the present. If not, he knows that he has chosen to make beliefs about the past or the future more important than being himself in the "the beginning." So he then, asks, "What is the false god that I am worshiping now?" It could be money, prestige, ego, meeting the expectations of another, false love, or unwillingness to say and do what is real. Those are all things that one might regret (which causes him to live in the past) or think he needs (which causes him to live the future.)

    Everyone needs money, for example, but one has the choice: find fulfillment in the moment and then seek what one needs, or seek what one needs to be fulfilled in the future. The latter strategy will never lead to fulfillment. It results in a vicious circle of upset, which Jesus calls "death."

- A Seeker knows that when living in the past or future, he is not embracing something or someone as "perfect-as-is." Instead, he is running from "bad" and seeking "good." He knows he must stop and embrace everything with unconditional love. That is the *only* way out of the mind-driven cycle of sadness to out-of-body bliss. We must transform deep anger about "bad" and not finding "good" into unconditional, pure love.

For example, a war veteran may suddenly feel terrible stress when his child drops something with a bang on the floor. Immediately that sound tells him that he is living the trauma of a battle where he experienced his friend being blown up. Thus, he knows that he has not embraced fully his friend, that situation, the enemy, the government, all, in unconditional love. His mind shouts, "believe that is bad." He knows that he cannot move forward until his being shouts, "It is perfect-as-is." But how to get there? He knows that only his soul knows his answer.

Therefore, he stops, goes apart from his family, and begs his soul, "Teach me."

He may be told to hold his child and think of his friend, the enemy, and the politicians who sent them to war as the soul essence of what he cherishes in his arms.

He may also be given the insight that he and everyone involved in that battle were brainwashed to kill in the name of some "good" false god.

He may be called to look at his hands and love his friend and his battlefield enemies with similar hands.

He may hear the suggestion to suffer not taking a drink of alcohol or swallowing another pill and to wait in pain for the answer to bubble up from his soul.

Every time this happens, his soul will say something different; each time tailoring the insight to his immediate need to leave his ego's demand that things were "bad."

Once he finds even the littlest bit of unconditional love for what is going on and/or what has gone on, his soul will prompt him to "guard" himself. He may do that by spending more time with his child, by listening to more gentle music, by using the internet to connect with others, by (any number of things). The soul knows the next step.

The only formula for healing is this: Unconditional love first, then guard. Seek "perfect-as-is" before using the mind to know the bad and good ways to move ahead safely. Never the reverse: thinking or acting out of "bad" and "good" hoping for unconditional love to follow is fruitless.

- A Seeker knows that universal intelligence (God), one with his soul, has led him into his present situation to *heal* him, to teach him to be unconditional-guarded love in the world. So he asks, "What am I to learn by this rejection, or by this misunderstanding, or by this problem, or by recalling that horrible event?" He waits to be shown how the *present situation* is his *next perfect step* to freedom from emotional trauma and to bring him to be a light leader in the world. He must learn to embrace what is going on, or he will just repeat it in other ways until he permits his soul to show him the way out.

To be clear: A Seeker *experiences* rather than *believes* that every thought, every urge, every thing that happens to him and around him happens to bring him to fulfillment in unconditional love guardedness. Those in the world experience or believe in bad and good luck and in coincidences. When one is one with his core self, fully in the "All Experience," he knows that everything going on is perfect-as-is and perfectly presents his next perfect step to fulfillment. Again, he does not live those things as blind beliefs, rather he seeks the All-Experience so that he will know them as obvious.

When a person has been shocked into dreading that he is vulnerable to be hurt or to die at any moment, he will live in "bad" and in perpetual anxiety and worry. The only way out is letting his source (Source) teach him personally how to live the Kingdom 24/7. He needs only to give up everything tying him to "bad" and "good" in order to be taught how to experience life correctly.

- A Seeker sees himself mirrored in everyone, particularly in his enemies. If he finds himself repulsed by anyone, he asks his soul, "What am I not embracing in love-guardedness in myself that I see in him?" "How is he me?" Or, if he notices the beauty of a kind person, he may ask, "Why did you, soul, bring him into my life?" "What are you teaching me?"

In short, the Seeker takes nothing for granted. It is all part of the cosmic lesson to bring him to being everything he deep-down desires—which Jesus' calls, the "kingdom." His goal is to be super-conscious of every thought and feeling. That will enable him to rule as king (or queen) over himself and his interaction with others. Then, he will be more the presence of unconditional love-guarded in the world.

- A Seeker seeks other Soul Seekers. Their souls will know each other beyond superficial differences. They will feel a love-guarded bond that will guide them to be family, even if just for a few minutes. Immediately, each soul will be communicating with the other and providing each other with learned lessons.

- Finally, a Seeker will discover that those who are not seekers of the kingdom will not understand him. Therefore, he will find that the only viable path to peace and sanity is to not rely on what Jesus calls "the world." That "world" may be long-time friends, family, a job, beliefs, money, material possessions, and so forth. A seeker of the kingdom sacrifices to obtain it all.

Appendix One

That, in a nutshell, is *one* way of understanding how immediately to practice the Way of the Soul.

Summary of the Two Ways

Here is a chart that comparatively summarizes and describes the characteristics of the Way of the Mind and the Way of the Soul:

The Two Ways Contrasted

Way of the Mind		Way of the Soul
Lives primarily from mind-knowing	→←	Lives primarily from soul-knowing
Indoctrinated	→←	Self-evolved
Divided between one's real self and many false selves	→←	United with oneself
In conflict with all others who differ in their religions and ideologies.	→←	In oneness with other people and the universe.
Develops faith in dogma	→←	Questions dogma to discover his own answers
Jesus call this Way: "Darkness," "death" and "sickness"	→←	Jesus calls this Way: "Light," "life" and "health"
The goal: Find meaning and security by attaching oneself to people, things and dogma	→←	The goal: Detach from people, things and dogma to wisely love all
Means: Think and imitate those you admire	→←	Means: Use your inner voice to decide for yourself how to think and act

Implications

- If a Soul person is in a relationship with a Mind person, they will psychologically separate. If they try to live together or be friends, they will both continually experience some degree of stress and disharmony.

- Religions institutionalize and normalize the Way of the Mind. They teach people to divide by labeling something, someone, or even parts of themselves as "bad" and "good." They teach people to identify with blind beliefs rather that with their core, beautiful, perfect-as-is souls. They teach adherents to live in fear of not getting into "heaven" or possibly going to "hell." In other words, they teach fear, that is, psychological illness. Religions teach people to "tolerate" people with contrary beliefs. Seekers know that withholding unconditional love by being tolerant is actually hate. Therefore, for all of those reasons, Seekers sever their allegiance to all secular and theological dogma-based institutions.

  Religions do not teach unconditional-guarded love of all. They do not empower people to use their souls to find their own answers. They, instead, indoctrinate and brainwash people to think and act according to official bad-good standards. Therefore, religions are the root cause of personal emotional problems and of inter-group political, social and national conflicts. They teach death logic as normal to the world. Jesus teaches the opposite.

- *Only* people *united* on the Way of the Soul will solve the horrific problems of overpopulation, competition for fewer resources, terrorism, global warming and the slew of plagues and crises facing humanity today.

- When we support, in any way, political, theological, economic, nationalistic or other social religions, we contribute to personal and inter-group conflicts, including horrific terrorism. When we identify with dogma, we divide from our core self and from others and become physically and mentally sick. Only allegiance to soul-knowing unites and heals. The world seeks salvation in new generations of weapons, in democracy, in justice systems, and in teaching tolerance. As history has shown, those solutions simply continue the cycle of hope to violence.

- Jesus did not build religious buildings or institutions, wear distinctive clothes, lead rituals to change one spiritually, establish a legalism or a creed, call himself anything special, discriminate against women and others, distinguish between spiritual and personal growth, ordain leaders with special powers, set up a hierarchy, or divide people into believers and non-believers. He did live in the "now," listening for the voice of his Mother and Father to guide him to love the person in front of him while protecting himself from that person's false identities. He did daily crucify himself of false selves to be resurrected to new levels of life, wisdom and fulfillment. He did communicate with God in his own way continually. He did empower everyone to find their own answers through soul-knowing. Thus, if he lived today, he would be unhappy if any group or individual associated him with dogma-religion that inevitably and automatically results in intrapersonal, interpersonal and inter-group conflict.

  As a person living the Way of the Soul, Jesus lived in the kingdom. It was not a nationalistic or ethnic kingdom, but a personal and group way of being. Through his teachings, we can see the life he lived and the life he intended for us to live. And through his words we can fulfill his wish for all of humanity—to live in the kingdom, on the Way of the Soul, together in peace.

One of Jesus' mantras that we can all say as we enter more and more into the Kingdom:

Chapter 16, Poem 10 (Saying 77)

I

am

the light

The one

Which

is

upon them

All of them.

I

am

the all;

Has

the all

come outward

of me

And

has

the all

split

to become me.

Split

a timber

And
I
am
there;

Take
the stone
up

And
you
will discover me
there.

Way of the Soul–Way of the Mind
Self-Examination

One of the characteristics of Jesus' Way of the Soul is self-examination. He says that in Chapter 16, Poem 2 (Saying 69a):

> The blest ones
>
> They
> are
> those
>
> Who
> have persecuted themselves
> in their own heart.
>
> Those
>
> Who
> have done that
>
> Have known the Father
> in truth.

The following exercise may enable you to "persecute" yourself so that you live more in "truth." To complete it, rate yourself, as honestly as you can, by checking the number below each of the factors that most closely matches your current life. (If you do this on your screen, write the numbers down on paper beside you).

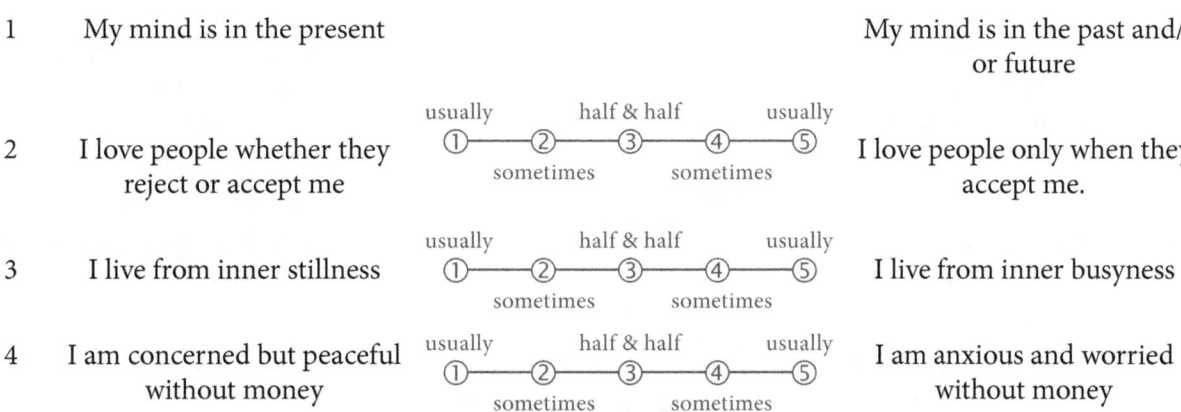

1	My mind is in the present		My mind is in the past and/ or future
2	I love people whether they reject or accept me		I love people only when they accept me.
3	I live from inner stillness		I live from inner busyness
4	I am concerned but peaceful without money		I am anxious and worried without money

5	I challenge and evolve my faith	usually ①—②—③—④—⑤ usually sometimes half & half sometimes	I ground myself in my firm, unchanging faith
6	I have "give and take" chats with my s(S)ource of inspiration	usually ①—②—③—④—⑤ usually sometimes half & half sometimes	I do not have "give and take" chats with my s(S)ource of inspiration
7	I live as me no matter what.	usually ①—②—③—④—⑤ usually sometimes half & half sometimes	I compromise myself to be accepted
8	I live in peace and joy.	usually ①—②—③—④—⑤ usually sometimes half & half sometimes	I live a roller-coaster life, from sadness to elation, from regret to worry, from anxiety to euphoria, on and on.
9	When someone turns me off, I seek to be more unconditionally loving of him and guarded.	usually ①—②—③—④—⑤ usually sometimes half & half sometimes	When someone turns me off, I move away from him and guard myself from him.
10	I seek feedback from others about how I can improve.	usually ①—②—③—④—⑤ usually sometimes half & half sometimes	I avoid feedback from others about how I can improve.
11	I enjoy sharing and hearing from another about the inner challenge to be more loving and alive.	usually ①—②—③—④—⑤ usually sometimes half & half sometimes	I like to keep conversations superficial and light.
12	I take only one vow—to be unconditional love guarded of all no matter the cost.	usually ①—②—③—④—⑤ usually sometimes half & half sometimes	I take vows to people, to groups, to my faith, to my flag, and to institutions.
13	I make nonseekers uncomfortable because I am unconventional and unpredictable.	usually ①—②—③—④—⑤ usually sometimes half & half sometimes	I make people comfortable because I am conventional and predictable.
14	I live from a loving, fierce s(S)pirit within me.	usually ①—②—③—④—⑤ usually sometimes half & half sometimes	I live from the general spirit of those around me.
15	I have a zeal for personal development.	usually ①—②—③—④—⑤ usually sometimes half & half sometimes	I seek the easy, familiar life.

Appendix Two

16	I become my best me in the moment, and then, respond with unconditional love- guarded to how I affect the world.	usually ①—②—③—④—⑤ usually sometimes half & half sometimes	I plan and control what happens around me, and then, deal with what I like and do not like.
17	When bad things happen, I seek to experience them as perfect-as-is before making changes.	usually ①—②—③—④—⑤ usually sometimes half & half sometimes	When bad things happen, I do what I can to make things good.
18	I am aware of all my thoughts and feelings.	usually ①—②—③—④—⑤ usually sometimes half & half sometimes	I do not pay attention to my thoughts and feelings.
19	I listen to anyone, but trust only my inner guidance.	usually ①—②—③—④—⑤ usually sometimes half & half sometimes	I trust peers, and authorities including those in scriptures more than I trust my inner guidance.
20	I am personally fulfilled.	usually ①—②—③—④—⑤ usually sometimes half & half sometimes	I am personally unfulfilled.
21	When unfulfilled, I use my soul-guidance to find fulfillment in the moment.	usually ①—②—③—④—⑤ usually sometimes half & half sometimes	When unfulfilled, I seek fulfillment "out there" in people and things.
22	I do not identify with anything but being unconditional love guarded in the world.	usually ①—②—③—④—⑤ usually sometimes half & half sometimes	I identify with my friends, country, family, race, things, money, religion and my other beliefs.
23	I relate to God only when I experience God.	usually ①—②—③—④—⑤ usually sometimes half & half sometimes	I believe or do not believe in God.
24	I welcome, confront, and conquer my inner turmoil.	usually ①—②—③—④—⑤ usually sometimes half & half sometimes	I seek outside relief from my inner turmoil through TV, drugs, alcohol, work, chatting, shopping, food, and other distractions.
25	I challenge social and religious norms until I am satisfied that they serve the highest ends.	usually ①—②—③—④—⑤ usually sometimes half & half sometimes	I trust that social and religious norms serve the highest ends.

26	I experience perfect, loving order behind all events.	usually ①—②—③—④—⑤ usually sometimes sometimes half & half	I experience good and bad luck, coinci-dences, that life is not fair, and that prayer may affect what happens.
27	I watch for how everything that happens offers me the next perfect step to becoming my fulfilled self.	usually ①—②—③—④—⑤ usually sometimes sometimes half & half	I dodge and weave through life avoiding bad things happening, regretting mistakes, and longing for what is missing.
28	I reveal my own personal truths (about who I am, what happens after I die, who others are, and life's other core questions) layer by layer, never getting to the core.	usually ①—②—③—④—⑤ usually sometimes sometimes half & half	Experts (clergy, professors, commentators, celebrities, and people I admire like Jesus, Mohammed, and other Scripture authors) teach me absolute truths about life's core questions.
29	Just like the authors of scriptures, I suspend my beliefs in order to be enlightened with higher truths.	usually ①—②—③—④—⑤ usually sometimes sometimes half & half	I am in awe of authors of scriptures who were chosen (unlike me) to be channels of God's truths.
30	I love surveys like this which help me decide how to improve.	usually ①—②—③—④—⑤ usually sometimes sometimes half & half	I hate surveys like this even though they are designed to help me improve.

Compute your score by adding your selected numbers and dividing by 30. Mark you score on the scale below.

usually ①—②—③—④—⑤ usually
sometimes   half & half   sometimes

Results: The lower your score, the more likely you are on the Way of the Soul. The higher your score, the more likely you are on the Way of the Mind. If Jesus walked his talk, his score would be very low.

APPENDIX THREE

The Evidence that Jesus Is the Author of The Gospel Thomas

Based on the organization and meaning of the Gospel of Thomas as I have described in this book, I believe we can infer some things about its author.

- The author was probably raised as a Jew and studied with Jewish sages. Based on what we know historically about the demographics of the region at the time of the writing, the concepts the author discusses, and the metaphors and allegories he uses, it is clear that he is deeply familiar with the Jewish culture and religion and Jesus' parables and sayings. For example, he knew the Old Testament metaphors, such as "kingdom" and "mountain," and the meaning of the allegories, such as that about the Garden of Eden and Moses' sojourn in the wilderness. He also had a thorough knowledge of Semitic Parallelism

- All of the poems express a single, consistent, cohesive way to personal/spiritual develop. This implies that a single author was primarily responsible for composing all of the Book's poems.

- Only a single author—one who deeply understood the meaning of the poems—could have composed the Gospel with so many interdependent levels of organization. It is hard to imagine two or more people with the knowledge and skills necessary to collaborate on such an elaborate, insightful project, and come up with such a cohesive, consistent work.

- The author was evolved in wisdom. The poems, individually and together as a cohesive work, have very deep meanings and are expressed in a timeless and general manner when looked at through the lens of the original organizational structure in which they were written and intended to be read. The author had no way of knowing that the way people read would change or how it would change over the centuries. The concepts, however, are enduring and do not become irrelevant as society and human experience changes. They imply a global, humanity-encompassing view of human experience which is generally only seen in those who have the ability to see both what is right in front of them and the "big picture."

- Because Semitic Parallelism was an oral compositional method and died out as writing became more mainstream, the author probably lived in the 1st or 2nd century.

- The author neither adhered to nor supported the Torah, the Jewish traditions, the Jewish authorities, or any other religious dogma.

- The author was a phenomenological poet, therapist and philosopher, not a logical, abstract theologian like Paul. The author studied people and nature and then arrived at the principles governing human interaction and evolution. He did not use his mind or mystical experiences to understand things that cannot be verified by others. He would never, for example, ask people to believe in the Trinity if that concept of God could not be experienced.

- The author of Thomas did follow the part of the Torah Books that describe the Way of Abraham. That Patriarch left his identity with his religion and traditions to follow the "voice" of God. He did not found a religion with a creed, buildings of worship, rituals, a legalism, a hierarchy of priests with special titles and clothes, or with the other things we associate with "religion." In other words, Moses founded Judaism, not Abraham. The author of the Gospel of Thomas expanded upon Abraham's Way and criticized the Way of Moses, and by extension, all other dogma-indoctrinating religions and ideological-based organizations.

- The author's philosophy is consistent with the New Testament parables that the Evangelists attribute to Jesus. He did not endorse anyone identifying with any theological or secular dogma. The author taught people to be guided by the will of God in every thought and action through soul-knowing (or third-eye and ear knowing).

- The author was a wise statesman. He saw that when large numbers of people identify with religious and secular dogma, cohesive, defensive, support groups form and ideas and rules of inclusion/exclusion and right/wrong develop. That causes division between individuals, groups and nations. Thus, he sought to bring oneness to the world by articulating a gospel based on people adhering to no dogma and following a common voice that that they know through soul-listening.

- The author likely expected that he might be killed, and may have experienced persecution because of his radical, anti-establishment message. Therefore, he probably composed the Gospel of Thomas to ensure that his message lived on and was available and accessible to humanity after he was gone.

- The author was a wise statesman. He saw that when large numbers of people identify with religious and secular dogma, groups form and ideas and rules of inclusion/exclusion and right/wrong develop. Division occurs within nations and between groups within them. Power struggles develop and humanity moves further away from peace. and the surrounding countries religious , in particular, and false gods. The author likely expected that he might be killed, and may have experienced persecution because of his radical, anti-establishment message and, therefore, composed the Gospel to ensure that his message lived on and was available and accessible to humanity after he was gone.

- The author knew that most people misinterpreted his poems and that few, if any, fully left their identifica-tion with their social and religious dogma to follow his "Way" of identifying only with his divine soul-life. Therefore, he expected that all or most of his followers would abandon him and his "Way" after he died. Therefore, he composed his poems according to Semitic Parallelism rules so that they could be interpreted correctly by future generations.

- The author was probably murdered. Palestine and the surrounding countries in the first and second century was ruled through an informal agreement between the Roman occupiers and their Jewish collaborators. They did not want an uprising to destroy that relationship and what it brought them. The Poems in Thomas criticize all indoctrinators and Jewish leaders by title. One would not live long in Palestine while publicly calling the elite "dogs" or false gods.

- If the author was murdered, his followers would have hidden his work after his death. They likely would have feared being caught with it, assuming they, too, would have been persecuted and killed. To save this Gospel, written copies would likely have been taken to a neighboring country, such as Syria or Egypt, where it could be protected and studied in relative safety. There, because of its radical message, it would likely have been disclosed to only a select few. Thus, this Gospel may have existed underground for more than a century after its composition.

- The author was not interested in self-importance. He did not make claims as to his importance compared to any other person's. He did not want to be anyone's master. He did not label himself as the Messiah or "the only Son of God." He desired only for people to honor the core divine life in themselves and others. He did everything possible to empower people to evolve in soul-knowing.

- The author lived love-guarded. He would have been a walking love-guard, and, as such, a perceived threat to everyone who wanted to continue to control populations through dogma and fear or who lived a life of dogma.

- The author would have affected people over great distances. He did not compose all of his poems in a single sitting. He would have composed one, edited it, recited it, and edited it again. He would have done that repeatedly until satisfied. Meanwhile, people would have memorized one poem after another as they were composed and communicated them to others, and they to others. In that way, over many years, knowledge of this wise person and his radical gospel would have spread over a great area, and likely to other countries when his poems were memorized and recited by traders and nomads. Therefore, when the author traveled, we would expect him to attract large crowds of friends and enemies. Further, after he died, we would expect that people in Palestine and in distant lands would recognize his name and poems and react positively or negatively to anyone preaching them.

- The author had a following of disciples and enemies. He lived these poems. He would have attracted people seeking the type of life and peace he spoke about and modeled, and he would have upset the conformists in the society around him. We would know about such an author. No-one with a large following of both disciples and enemies, and with such a huge portfolio of poems, with such a radical message, could have remained unmentioned in the writings of that time or completely vanish from the historical record.

- One does not leave the Way of the Mind to follow the Way of the Soul quickly or easily. It takes courage and time. It is reasonable to expect that few, if any, truly grasped his radical message right away. And, making it more difficult for people to transform themselves in the first and second centuries, economic conditions were very difficult and the average life expectancy was about 35 years. Few people would have had the time and luxury of abandoning their preoccupation with survival in order to live his Way. Further, we would expect that after the author died, many convenient versions of his message would form the basis of competing communities. Each would find some way to keep their traditions and sacred dogma rather than abandon all to follow the Way of the Soul.

Conclusion

When considering all of these (what I strongly believe to be) reasonable facts and inferences, the only person documented in history whose story matches the entire list is Jesus. He wrote the Gospel of Thomas.

APPENDIX FOUR

Was Jesus The Expected Messiah

Recall, the word "Messiah" comes from the Hebrew word "mashiach" and means "anointed one" or "chosen one." Many people were "anointed" in the Old Testament. However, some prophesies pointed to two special ones who would appear that would bring peace to Israel and the world. We read in Zech. 6:13:

> It is he who shall build the temple of the Lord and shall bear royal honor, and shall sit and rule on his throne. And, there shall be a priest beside him on his throne, and the counsel of peace shall be between them both.

This passage speaks of the King Messiah, who will "build the temple" and "rule on his throne," and the Priest Messiah would be "beside him." Because we are told that "a counsel of peace shall be between them both," we know that they would be using the same principles to govern.

The First Holy Temple in Jerusalem was built in 957 B.C.E. by King Solomon, and was destroyed by the Babylonians in 587 B.C.E. The Second Temple was authorized by Cyrus the Great and constructed under the auspices of the Jewish governor Zerubbabel. It was dedicated in 515 B.C.E., and renovated by Herod the Great around 20 B.C.E. It was destroyed by the Roman Empire in 70 C.E. Jesus was clearly not involved with the construction of the Holy Temple. As a result, many believe this precludes Jesus as the Messiah.

Many interpret "It is he who shall build the temple of the Lord" to mean, "It is he who will cleanse the temple of false teachings." While the canonical Gospels describe Jesus "cleansing" the Temple (John 2:13–16; Matthew 21:12–13; Mark 11:15–17; Luke 19:45–46), it was not a wholesale cleansing of false teachings that is described. So again, consequently, many do not regard him as the Messiah.

However, in many of Jesus' poems and parables, he points to the "place" from which we live and communicate directly with God. For example, in Chapter 2, Poem 4 we read:

> He
> will delay
> not
>
> Namely
> the man
> of maturity
> in his days

> To ask a little
> small child
>
> He
> being
> of seven days
>
> About the place
> of life;
>
> And
> he
> will live.

That "place" within seems to be the "temple." Thus, Jesus builds that temple by teaching people to rediscover that "place" of "life" and to make it all important, especially when communicating directly with God. In that way, he does fulfill the prophesy about the Messiah.

"It is he ... who shall bear royal honor, and shall sit and rule on his throne." The Messiah will possess a regal demeanor and power. He will "rule" by both the force of his personality and by the authority given to him by others (many think by the entire world). Since Jesus was a humble man with noble but not regal character, he was not recognized as a ruler.

"And, there shall be a priest beside him on his throne." Many interpret that statement to mean that there will be two Messiahs who will redeem the world—a King Messiah and a Priest Messiah.

Zechariah does not imply that the King Messiah would be greater than the Priest Messiah. Other ancient documents, such as the Testament of Levi in the Dead Sea Scrolls, seem to indicate that the priest will be wiser and the king will be more visible and assertive. Zechariah also does not imply that the two Messiahs will be alive at the same time. "Beside him" can also mean "on the same Way," not literally "at his physical side." The Priest could create the wisdom that the King administers later, which would be a logical progression.

In Jewish eschatology (theology concerned with the final events of history, or the ultimate destiny of humanity), the Priest Messiah is known as "Mashiach ben Joseph" (Messiah son of Joseph; Joseph, the son of Jacob). The King Messiah has come to be known as "Mashiach ben David" (Messiah son of David). The phrase "son of" does not necessarily mean genetic lineage. It could mean "one who has inherited the spirit, charisma or character of someone who lived previously."

Let us suppose that the Priest Messiah arrives before the King Messiah. Recall the following passage from the Preface:

> He shall judge between the nations,
> and shall decide for many peoples;
> and they shall beat their swords into plowshares,
> and their spears into pruning hooks;
> nation shall not lift up sword against nation,
> neither shall they learn war any more. (Isa. 2:4)
>
> For every warrior's sandal from the noisy battle
> and their garments rolled in blood
> will be burned as fuel for the fire.
> For a child has been born,
> a son has been given...
> And his name shall be called
> Prince of Peace...
> Of the abundance of his government and peace
> there shall be no end (Isa. 9:5-10)

"His name shall be called Prince of Peace." In order for a Messiah to bring peace to a world where most people are on the Way of the Mind, he would need to preach an alternative Way that everyone, including Atheists and Agnostics, could embrace. Further, this new "Way" would be a type of emotional health system that would heal a person divided between his real and false selves. We saw, explained in this book, that Jesus taught people to put all of their belief in doctrines aside and listen only to their soul voice for their guidance. As we discovered, Jesus proclaimed the Way of the Soul. For most people, that is a paradigm-shift message that will unite people personally and globally. Thus, Jesus *does* fulfill the prophesy for the Priest Messiah.

However, Jesus did not "judge between the nations" and compel them "to beat their swords into plowshares" so that "nation shall not lift up sword against nation." Nor did he lead "abundance" of world-wide "government." The world continues to be torn apart by strife and war. Therefore, if Zechariah is correct, the King Messiah will do what Jesus—as the first, Priest Messiah—did not, and will certainly govern with the gospel of the Priest Messiah: the Way of the Soul.

The fulfillment of Isaiah's prophecy—that a Messiah could proclaim a way of living that would *replace* every form of religion and ideology—seems utterly impossible.

Jeremiah explains the role of the Priest Messiah further:

> But this is the covenant which I will make with the house of Israel after those days, says the Lord: I will put my law within them, and I will write it upon their hearts; and I will be their God, and they shall be my people. And no longer shall each man teach his neighbor and each his brother, saying, `Know the Lord,' for they shall all know me, from the least of

them to the greatest, says the Lord; for I will forgive their iniquity, and I will remember their sin no more. (Jer. 31: 33-34)

"But this is the covenant which I will make with the house of Israel." The "house of Israel" are the "family," "friends," and "descendants" of Israel (Jacob): those who are on the Way of the Soul. Thus, Jeremiah predicts that there will be a new covenant (promise) to those who follow the Messiahs, almost certainly on the Way of the Soul.

"I will put my law within them, and I will write it upon their hearts; and I will be their God, and they shall be my people." A Priest Messiah will teach people the natural laws of God. Those laws will be recognized in and come from their "hearts," not from any external authority or dogma. Religious and secular authorities and their dogmas will no longer be their rulers. Instead, the God who guides them through soul-knowing will be their authority.

In the Gospel of Thomas, Jesus taught the "law within" people, not the Torah laws of Moses or any other external, man-constructed law. Further, he presented the danger of making any secular or religious laws more important than what is in a person's heart and soul. Therefore, Jesus as the Priest Messiah fulfilled Jeremiah's requirements.

Ezekiel also prophesized the characteristics of the Messiah:

> Thus says the Lord God: "Behold, I will take the people of Israel from the nations among which they have gone, and will gather them from all sides, and bring them to their own land; and I will make them one nation in the land, upon the mountains of Israel.
>
> And one king shall be king over them all; and they shall be no longer two nations, and no longer divided into two kingdoms.
>
> They shall not defile themselves any more with their idols and their detestable things, or with any of their transgressions; but I will save them from all the dwelling places in which they have sinned, and will cleanse them; and they shall be my people, and I will be their God.
>
> My servant David will be king over them, and they will all have one shepherd. They will follow my laws and be careful to keep my decrees.
> (Eze. 37: 21-24)

"Thus says the Lord God: 'Behold, I will take the people of Israel from the nations among which they have gone, and will gather them from all sides, and bring them to their own land; and I will make them one nation in the land, upon the mountains of Israel.'" Let's explore this in detail.

"I will take the people of Israel." "Israel" is the name given to Jacob (the grandson of Abraham) after he wrestled with an angel (his soul knowing) to conquer himself. Thus, "people of Israel" does not mean citizens of the state of Israel or the literal descendants of Israel (Jacob). Instead, the statement refers to those on the Way of the Soul, like Israel, who wrestle with their soul knowing every day.

"I will take the people of Israel from the nations." "The nations" are what Jesus calls the "world." They are those on the Way of the Mind.

"I will gather them from all sides, and bring them to their own land; and I will make them one nation in the land, upon the mountains of Israel." "I will gather all people, from everywhere, and bring them each to their own soul knowing; and I will make them into a new, singular nation, together in soul knowing, with all of those who are already on their internal mountain—the highest place within themselves, free of distraction from or adherence to former beliefs."

A "land" is a "way of being" (soul knowing), which Jesus called the "kingdom." A person on the Way of the Soul establishes himself as a king or queen over himself and his interactions with others, that is, over his "kingdom."

The physical land of King David is now divided between many Jewish factions and between Jews and Palestinians and their many factions. That physical "land" will be united by the Messiah, which has not happened. So Jesus, as the first Messiah, did not fulfill the prophesy.

However, should everyone in the physical land of King David become one on the Way of the Soul as a result of the second Messiah's leadership, then the prophesy would be fulfilled in two ways:

First: The people living in the physical land of King David would be united.

Second: Everyone on the Way of the Soul throughout the world would become "one nation" in soul living.

"I will make them one nation in the land upon the mountains of Israel." I will make them one because they will all be listening to the same soul voice when they go up on their inner mountain.

"And one king shall be king over them all; and they shall be no longer two nations, and no longer divided into two kingdoms." Because all of those on the Way of the Mind will convert to the Way of the Soul, the Messiah King shall rule all as a single entity. And each person will be fully on the Way of the Soul, connected to his true self, with no false selves to "divide him into two kingdoms." All will be united on the Way of the Soul.

They shall not defile themselves any more with their idols and their detestable things, or with any of their transgressions; but I will save them from all the back-slidings in which they have sinned, and will cleanse them; and they shall be my people, and I will be their God." They will not defile their true selves by attempting to "ride two horses" or move between the Way of the Soul and the Way of the Mind. They will no longer be concerned with or distracted by those material and dogmatic things that prevent them from soul living.

"My servant David will be king over them, and they will all have one shepherd." The King Messiah will be the king and shepherd over those on the Way of the Soul.

"They will follow my laws and be careful to keep my decrees." They will follow God's laws that are within them in their hearts and soul knowing, not religious or secular laws. They will listen to and follow the guidance of God from within.

Conclusion

Jesus was the Priest Messiah who articulated the Way of the Soul. We find it completely in the Gospel of Thomas, and we find it also in his parables and core sayings in the New Testament.

The King Messiah has not yet come. When he does, he will proclaim compellingly to the world the Way of the Soul.

APPENDIX TWO

ACKNOWLEDGEMENTS

An author's name is on the front of the book. He does do the bulk of the work; however, in most cases, and this is one, he could not have done it without the support of others.

This book is the fruit of 18 years of idea hoeing, planting, weeding, pruning, and harvesting. I worked the first five years alone in a cabin in the desert outside Santa Fe, New Mexico. I may have gone crazy and given up if it were not for three people: my brother Don continued to check in on me from New York, Charlie Leavitt provided encouragement and offered me training gigs, and Joe Rook, my first editor, reviewed and revised every idea and page. Their almost weekly emails and calls were a lifeline to reality.

I then, moved to Mexico and met my wife, Carmen. She and her five children (Cristina, Alejandra, Francesca, Carmelita and Alejandro) have been supportive for 10 years without understanding much about Biblical scholarship.

Along the way, other editors have helped immensely:

- Bruce Klippenstein,
- Brandon Phillips,
- Aundria Warren, and
- Ruth Cohen.

Others contributed greatly:

My friend Marvin Baker and Linda Klippenstein who were most helpful through some difficult times in Mexico.

Jeff Chase, Gwen Boucher, Ed Krause, Paul D'Heilly, and William Lynch, all of whom said, "I believe in you and this project."

People from the past came forward with their support:

My former high school friend, Jack Ewers;

Two former Jesuit buddies, Jack Linn and Norm Betz;

My cousin/sister, Nancy Parzych, the best there is, who kept writing to say that she could not understand why anyone would be interested, but that she was behind me,

My brothers Terry and Rick, and my son Mike.

Raul, a poor but rich man, living high in the mountain village of Terrero, Guanajuato who helped with his friendship, music and anything else that he had,

Dan Mantz, who, without understanding much, said, "Sounds good, go live in my vacant house near the beach,"

William Gower and Paul de Heilly, who helped with the book's final production, and

My wonderful friends, Don Talarico, who established the book's style and discussed every poem, and Steve Mitchell who conceived of the phrases "Way of the Soul" and "Way of the Mind."

And most especially: The adult/child and the little child that guided and inspired me:

In Chapter 2, Poem 3 (Saying4) Jesus states that a wise person will humble himself to seek the "place of life" in a little child. For eleven years, Carmen Peraza has been that adult-child model for me as she tended to my every need. She has been a wonderful companion as she brought her brood of children and grand children into my life, including Amy.

www.ingramcontent.com/pod-product-compliance
Lightning Source LLC
Chambersburg PA
CBHW060422010526
44118CB00017B/2326